EASY GUITAR WITH NOTES & TAB

BEST OF R.E.M.

T0086583

Cover photograph by Laura Levine

ISBN 978-1-4768-6784-7

HAL•LEONARD® CORPORATION

7777 W. BLUEMOUND RD. P.O. BOX 13819 MILWAUKEE, WI 53213

In Australia Contact:
Hal Leonard Australia Pty. Ltd.
4 Lentara Court
Cheltenham, Victoria, 3192 Australia
Email: ausadmin@halleonard.com.au

Visit Hal Leonard Online at
www.halleonard.com

STRUM AND PICK PATTERNS

This chart contains the suggested strum and pick patterns that are referred to by number at the beginning of each song in this book. The symbols ⊓ and ∨ in the strum patterns refer to down and up strokes, respectively. The letters in the pick patterns indicate which right-hand fingers play which strings.

p = thumb
i = index finger
m = middle finger
a = ring finger

For example; Pick Pattern 2
is played: thumb - index - middle - ring

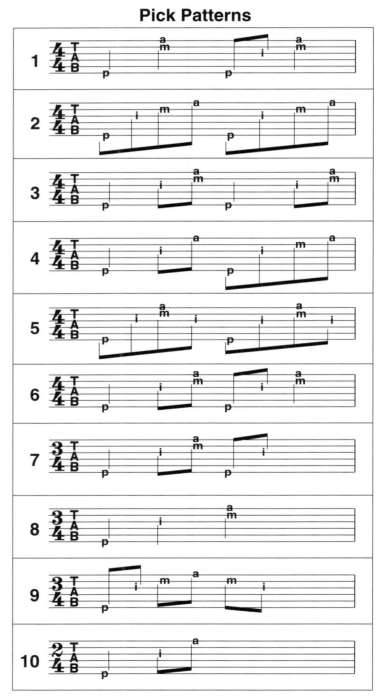

Strum Patterns   **Pick Patterns**

You can use the 3/4 Strum and Pick Patterns in songs written in compound meter (6/8, 9/8, 12/8, etc.).
For example, you can accompany a song in 6/8 by playing the 3/4 pattern twice in each measure.
The 4/4 Strum and Pick Patterns can be used for songs written in cut time (¢) by doubling the note time values in the patterns. Each pattern would therefore last two measures in cut time.

Drive

Words and Music by William Berry, Peter Buck, Michael Mills and Michael Stipe

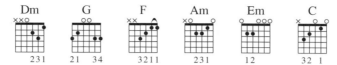

Strum Pattern: 3, 6
Pick Pattern: 3, 6

No - bod - y tells you where to go, ___ ba - by.
May - be you're cra - zy in the head, ___ ba - by.
No - bod - y tells you where to go, ___ ba - by.

Chorus

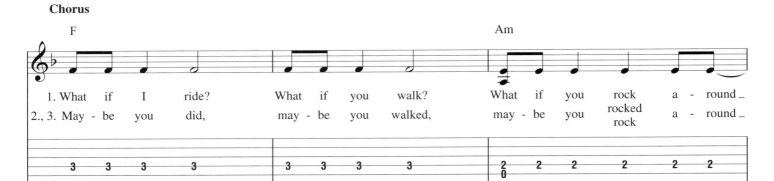

1. What if I ride? What if you walk? What if you rock a - round ___
2., 3. May - be you did, may - be you walked, may - be you rocked a - round ___
rock

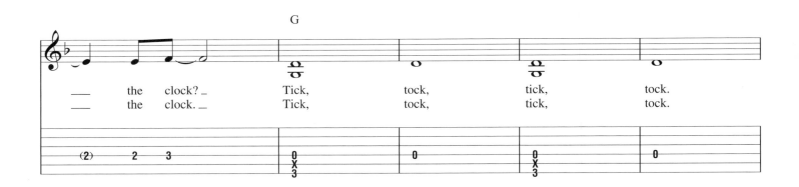

___ the clock? __ Tick, tock, tick, tock.
___ the clock. __ Tick, tock, tick, tock.

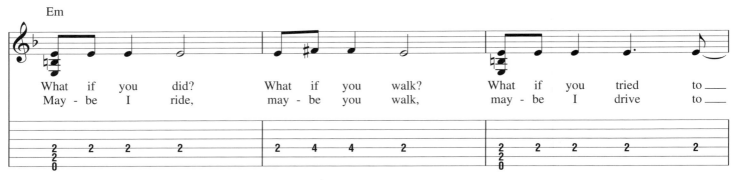

What if you did? What if you walk? What if you tried to ___
May - be I ride, may - be you walk, may - be I drive to ___

get off, ___ ba - by?
get off, ___ ba - by.

To Coda ⊕
Bridge
C

Hey, kids,

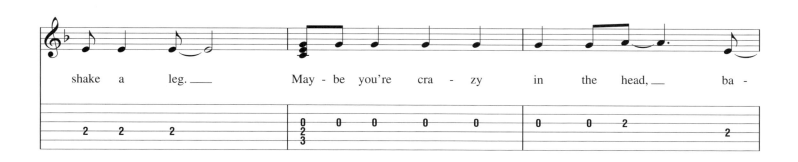

shake a leg. ___ May - be you're cra - zy in the head, ___ ba -

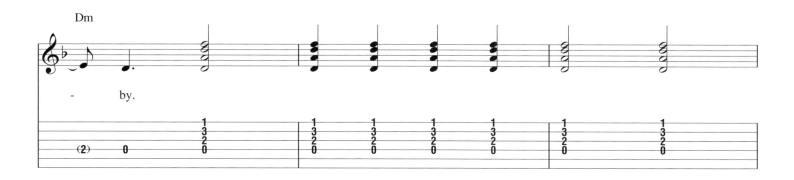

- by.

C

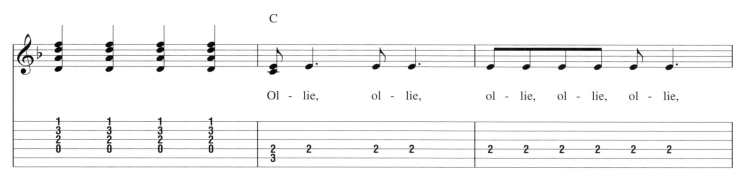

Ol - lie, ol - lie, ol - lie, ol - lie, ol - lie,

ol - lie, ol - lie, in come free, ba - by.

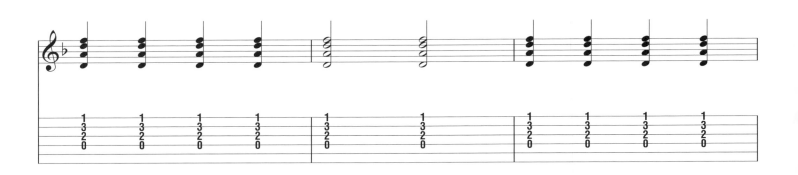

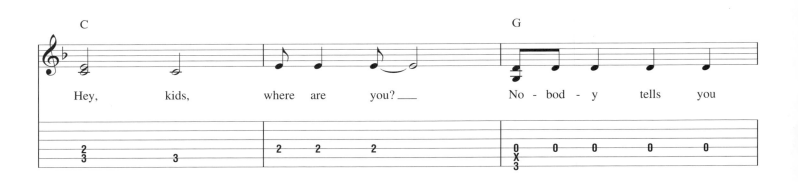

Hey, kids, where are you? ___ No - bod - y tells you

what to do, ___ ba - by.

Coda

Em

Hey, kids, where are you?___ No - bod - y tells you
Hey, kids, where rock and roll.___ No - bod - y tells you

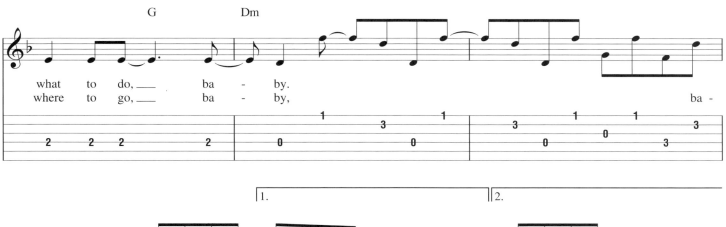

G   Dm

what to do,___ ba - by.
where to go,___ ba - by,   ba -

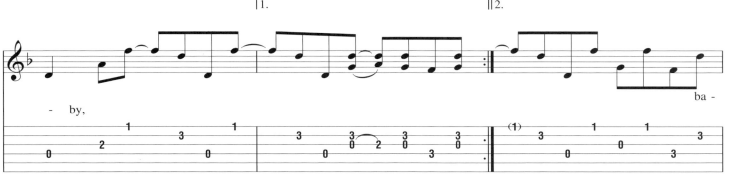

1.   2.

- by,   ba -

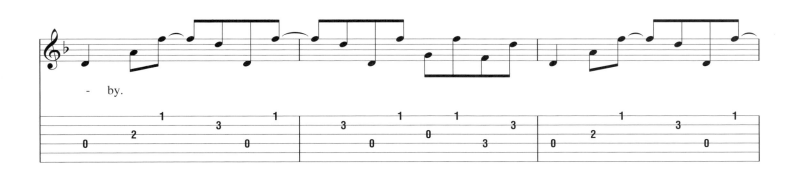

- by.

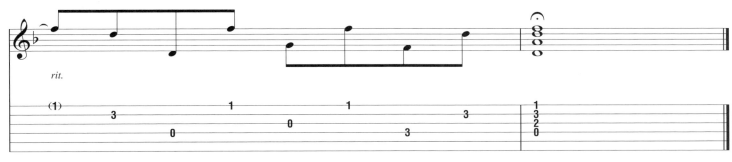

rit.

Everybody Hurts

Words and Music by William Berry, Peter Buck, Michael Mills and Michael Stipe

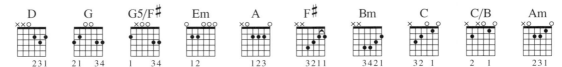

Strum Pattern: 8
Pick Pattern: 8

Intro
Slow, in 2

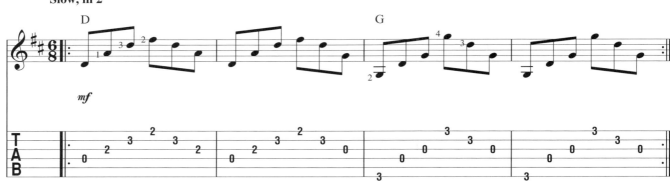

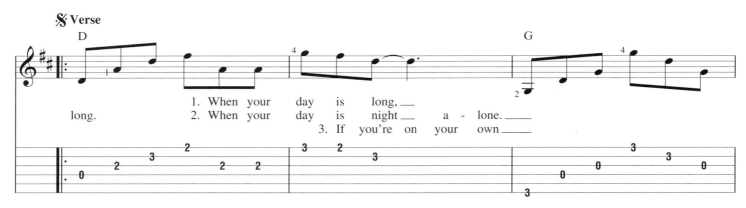

1. When your day is long, ___
2. When your day is night ___ a - lone. ___
3. If you're on your own ___

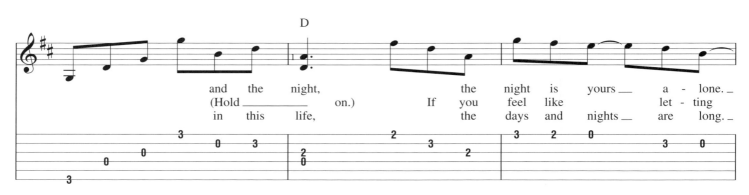

and the night, the night is yours ___ a - lone. ___
(Hold _____ on.) If you feel like let - ting
in this life, the days and nights ___ are long. ___

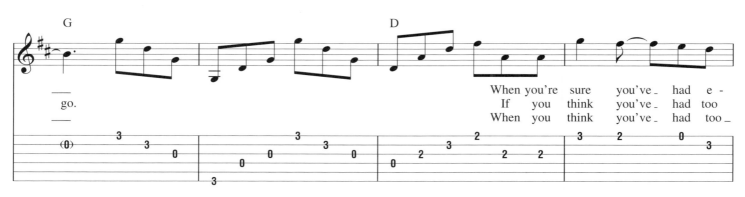

___ go.   When you're sure you've ___ had e -
___ If you think you've ___ had too
When you think you've ___ had too ___

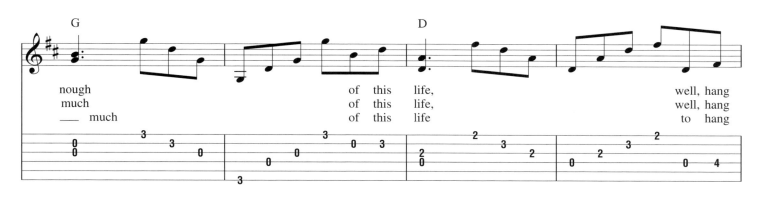

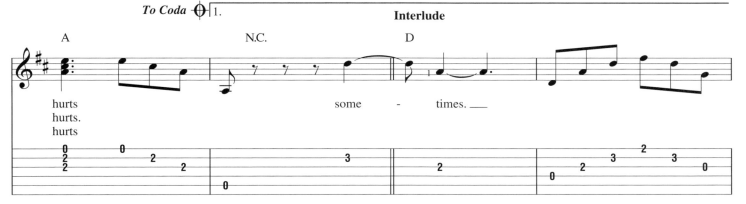

9

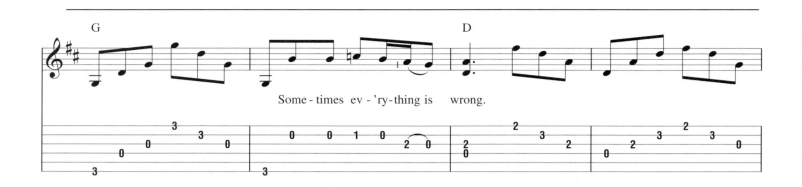

Some-times ev-'ry-thing is wrong.

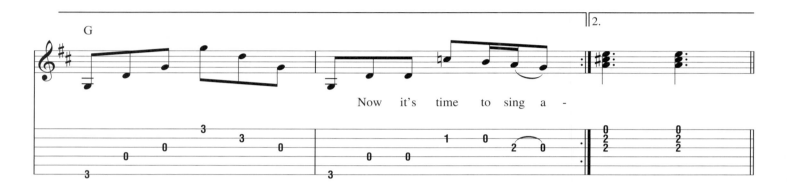

Now it's time to sing a -

Bridge

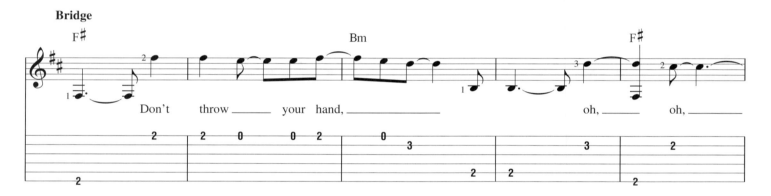

Don't throw _____ your hand, _____ oh, _____ oh, _____

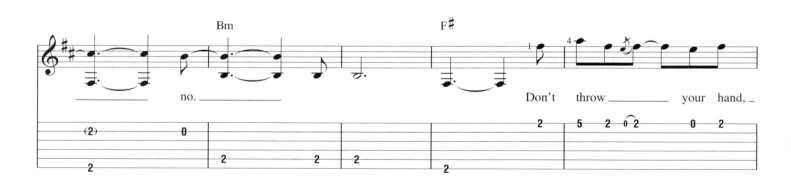

_____ no. _____ Don't throw _____ your hand, _

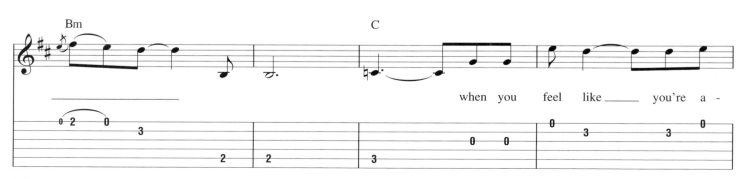

when you feel like _____ you're a -

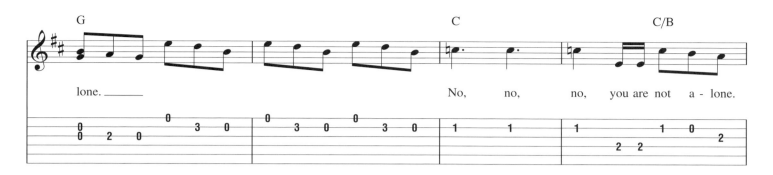

lone. _____ No, no, no, you are not a‑lone.

D.S. al Coda

◆ **Coda**

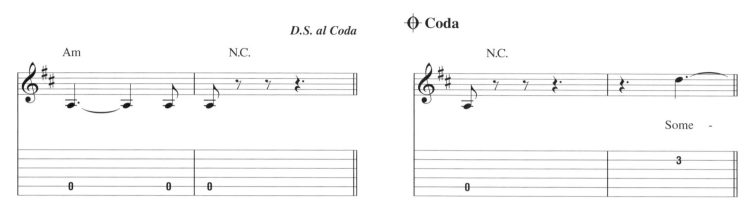

Some -

Outro

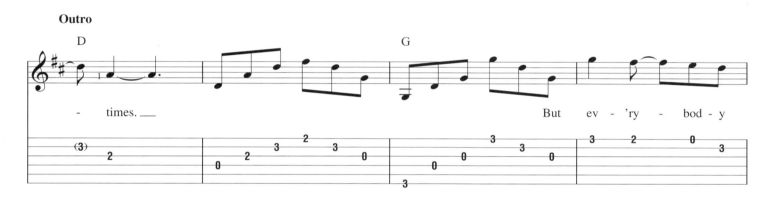

- times. ___ But ev‑'ry‑bod‑y

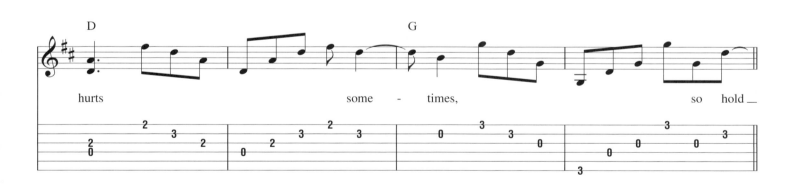

hurts some‑times, so hold __

Repeat and fade

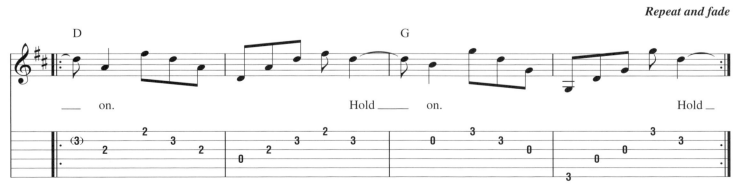

__ on. Hold ___ on. Hold _

Imitation of Life

Words and Music by Peter Buck, Michael Mills and Michael Stipe

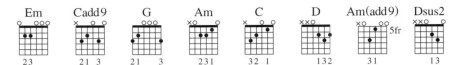

*Strum Pattern: 5
*Pick Pattern: 5

Intro
Moderately

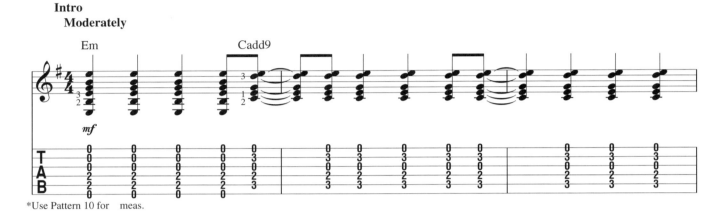

*Use Pattern 10 for meas.

Verse

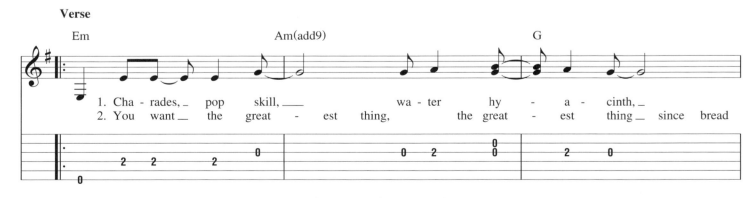

1. Cha - rades, _ pop skill, ___ wa - ter hy - a - cinth, _
2. You want _ the great - est thing, the great - est thing _ since bread

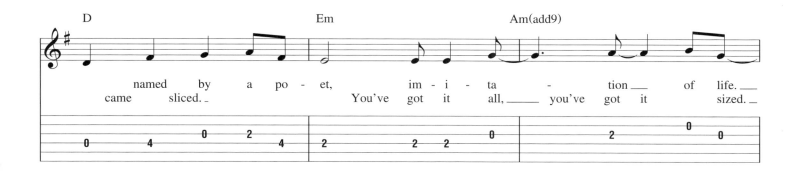

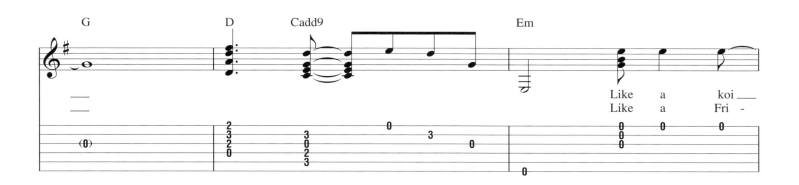

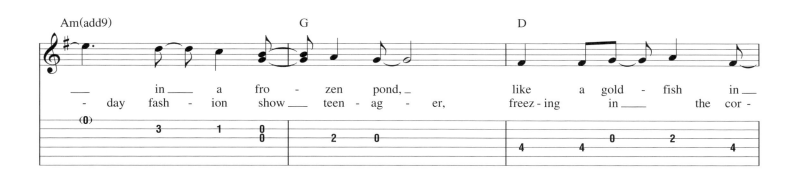

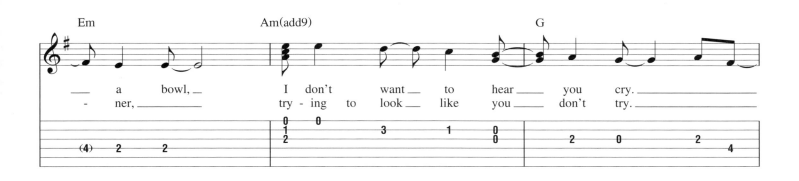

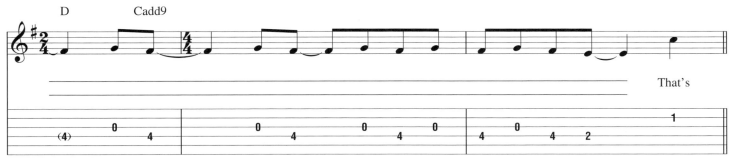

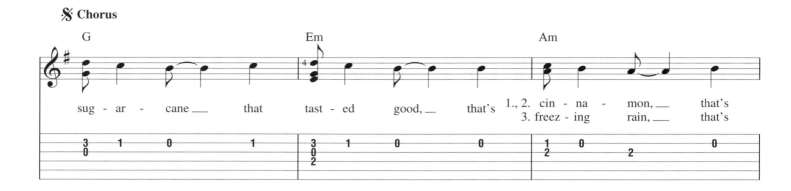

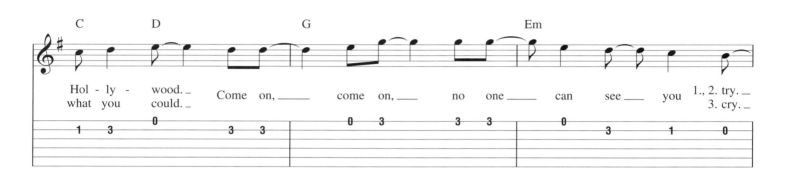

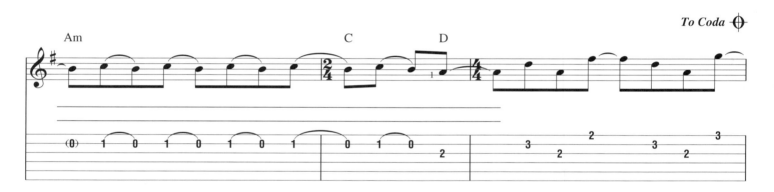

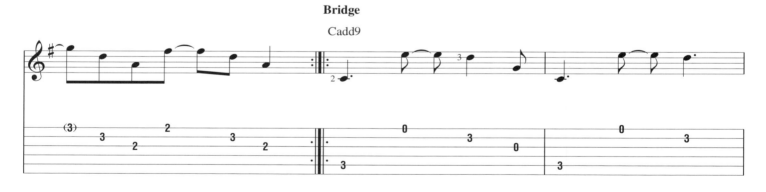

Bridge

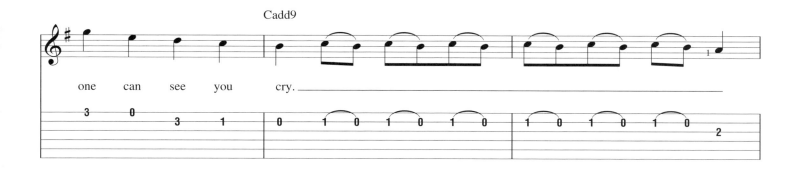

one can see you cry. _____

D.S. al Coda   ⊕ **Coda**

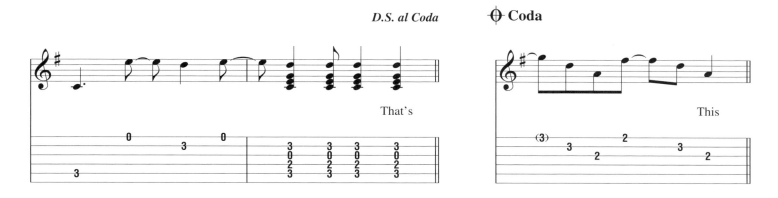

That's   This

Chorus

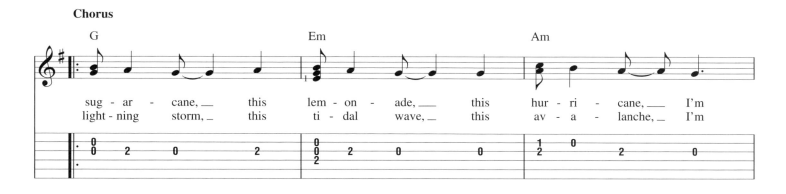

sug - ar - cane, __ this lem - on - ade, __ this hur - ri - cane, __ I'm
light - ning storm, _ this ti - dal wave, __ this av - a - lanche, __ I'm

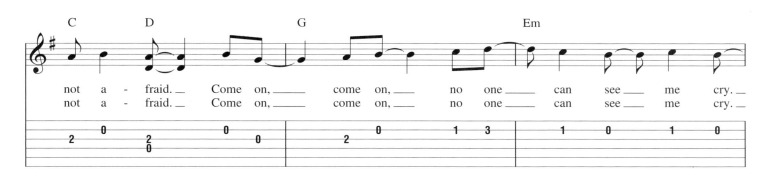

not a - fraid. __ Come on, _____ come on, ___ no one _____ can see ___ me cry. __
not a - fraid. __ Come on, _____ come on, ___ no one _____ can see ___ me cry. __

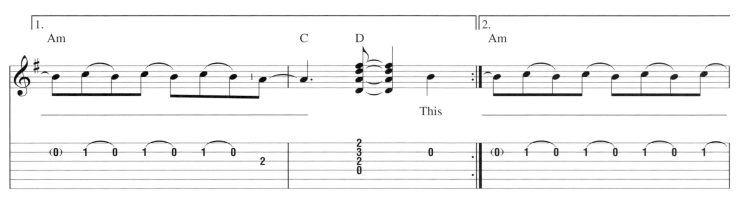

This

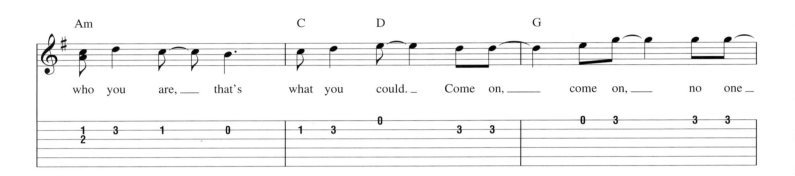

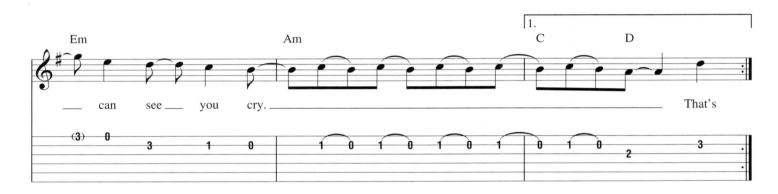

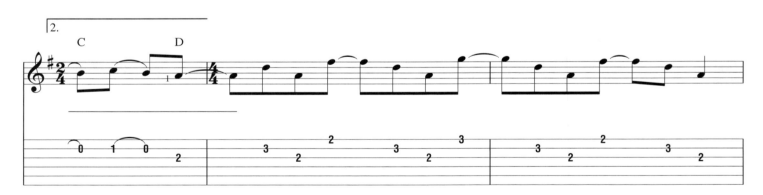

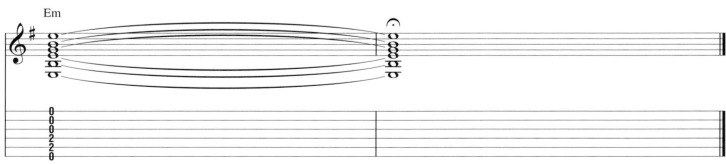

It's the End of the World as We Know It

Words and Music by William Berry, Peter Buck, Michael Mills and Michael Stipe

Verse

2. Left her, was-n't com-ing in a hur-ry with the fur-ies breath-ing down your
3. Six o'-clock, T V hour. Don't get caught in for-eign tow-er. Slash and burn, re-turn,

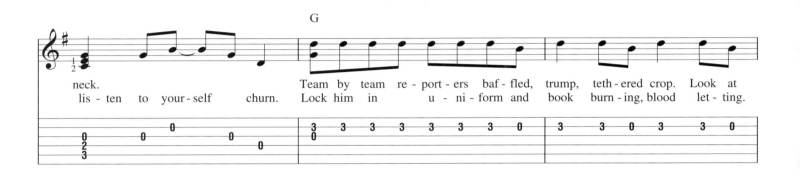

neck.
lis-ten to your-self churn. Team by team re-port-ers baf-fled, trump, teth-ered crop. Look at
Lock him in u-ni-form and book burn-ing, blood let-ting.

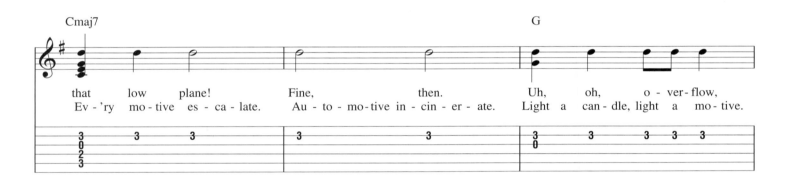

that low plane! Fine, then. Uh, oh, o-ver-flow,
Ev-'ry mo-tive es-ca-late. Au-to-mo-tive in-cin-er-ate. Light a can-dle, light a mo-tive.

pop-u-la-tion, com-mon group, but it-'ll do. Save your-self, serve your-self. World serve its
Step down, step down. Watch a heel crush, crush. Uh, oh, this means

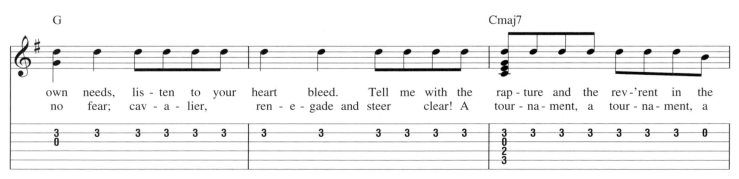

own needs, lis-ten to your heart bleed. Tell me with the rap-ture and the rev-'rent in the
no fear; cav-a-lier, ren-e-gade and steer clear! A tour-na-ment, a tour-na-ment, a

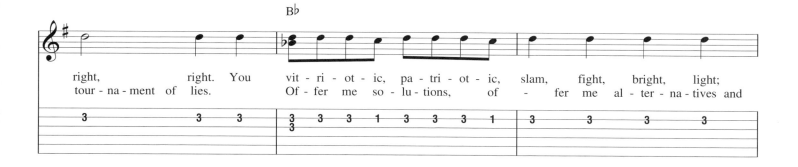

right,   right. You vit - ri - ot - ic, pa - tri - ot - ic, slam, fight, bright, light;
tour - na - ment of lies.   Of - fer me so - lu - tions, of - fer me al - ter - na - tives and

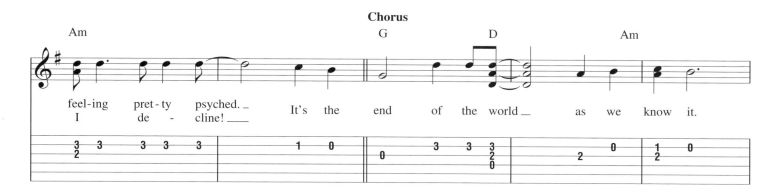

Chorus

feel-ing pret - ty psyched.   It's the end of the world as we know it.
I de - cline! ___

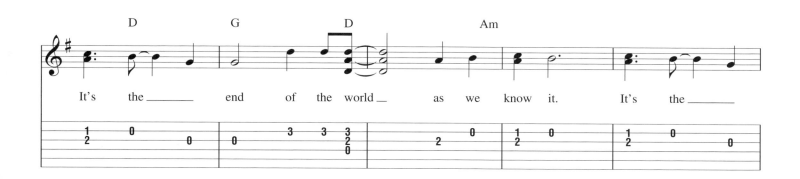

It's the _____ end of the world as we know it.   It's the _____

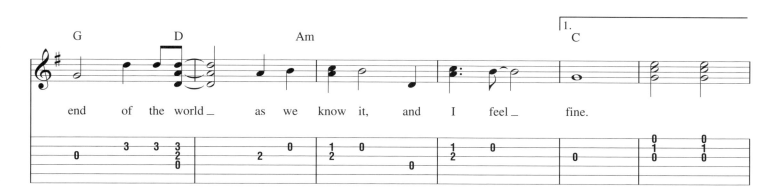

|1.

end of the world as we know it, and I feel fine.

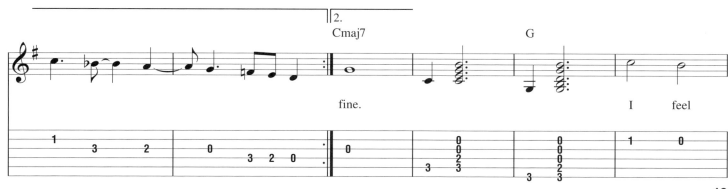

|2.

fine.   I feel

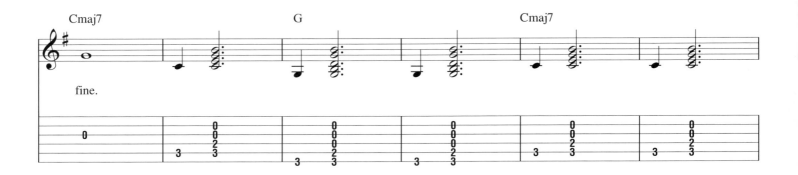

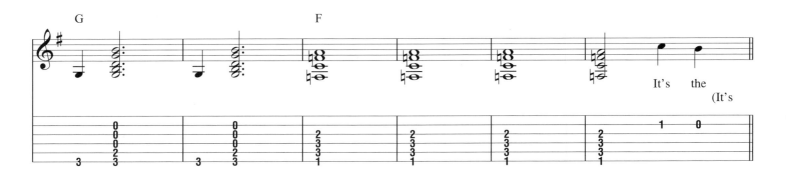

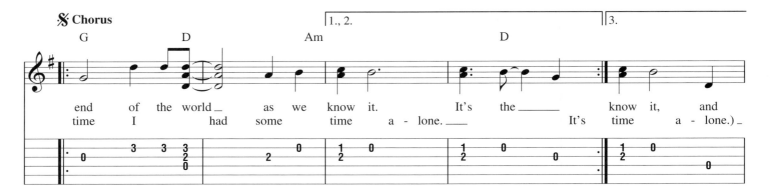

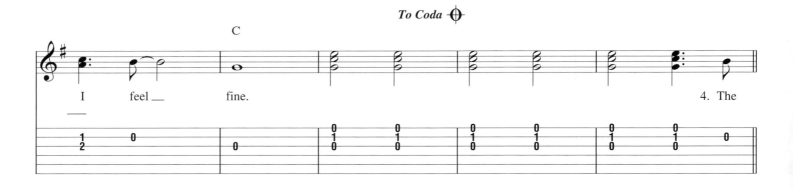

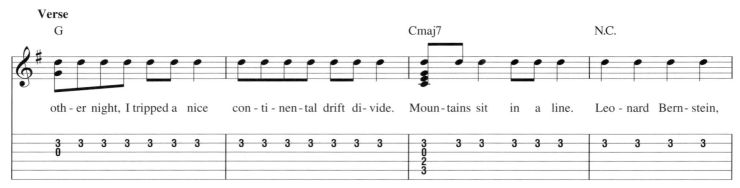

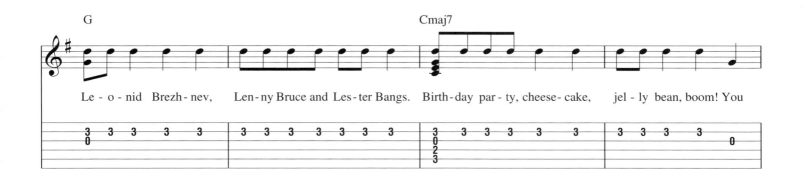

Le - o - nid Brezh - nev, Len - ny Bruce and Les - ter Bangs. Birth-day par - ty, cheese- cake, jel - ly bean, boom! You

D.S. al Coda
(take repeats)

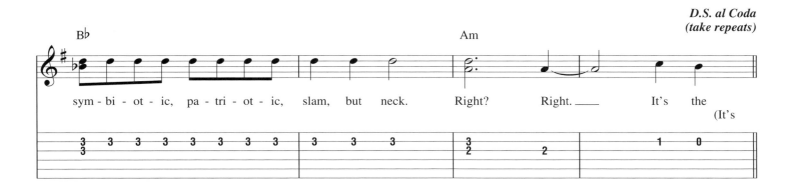

sym - bi - ot - ic, pa - tri - ot - ic, slam, but neck. Right? Right. ___ It's the
(It's

⊕ **Coda**

It's the

𝄋 𝄋 **Chorus**

|1., 2. |3.

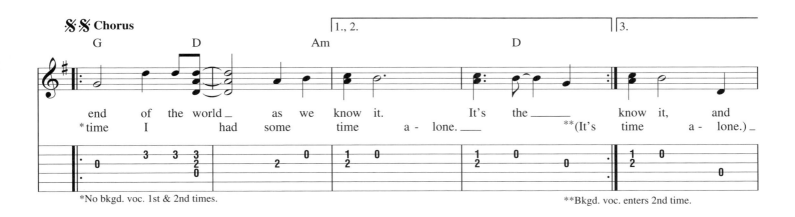

end of the world ___ as we know it. It's the ___ know it, and
*time I had some time a - lone. ___ **(It's time a - lone.) _

*No bkgd. voc. 1st & 2nd times.   **Bkgd. voc. enters 2nd time.

D.S.S. and fade
(take repeats)

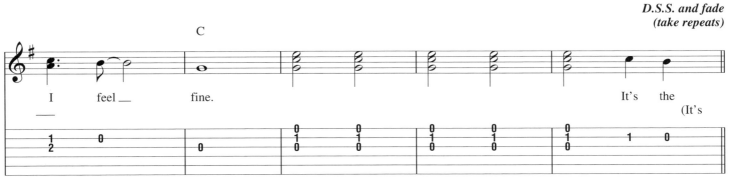

I feel ___ fine.   It's the
(It's

21

Losing My Religion

Words and Music by William Berry, Peter Buck, Michael Mills and Michael Stipe

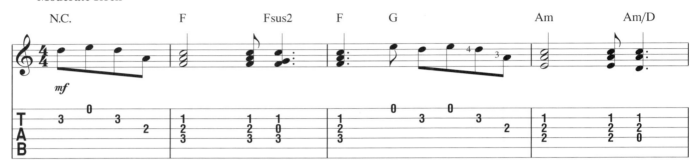

Strum Pattern: 2
Pick Pattern: 4

Intro

Moderate Rock

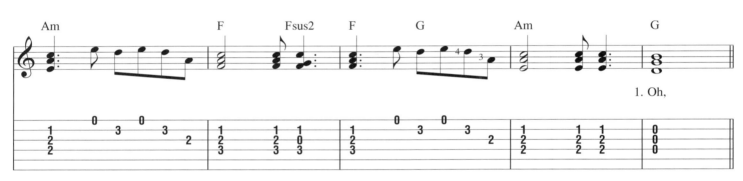

1. Oh,

Verse

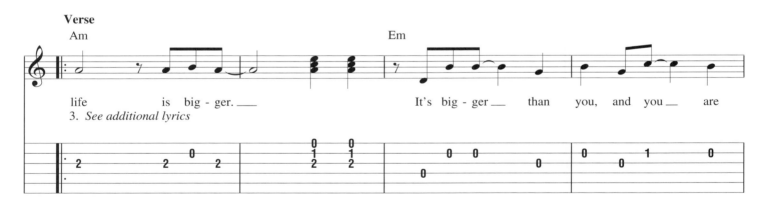

life   is big - ger. ___   It's big - ger ___ than you, and you ___ are
3. *See additional lyrics*

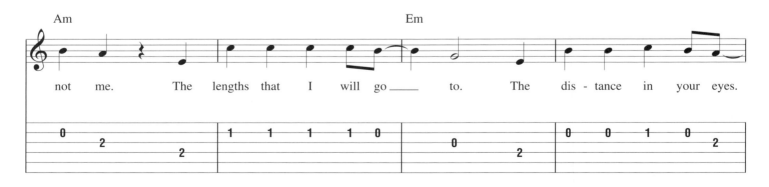

not me.   The lengths that I will go ___ to.   The dis - tance in your eyes.

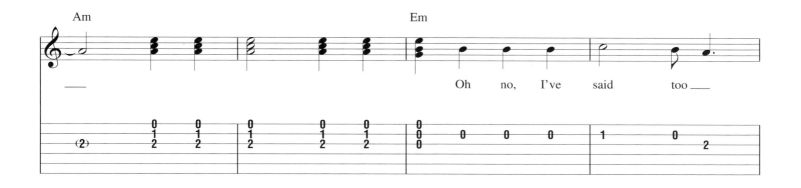

Oh no, I've said too ___

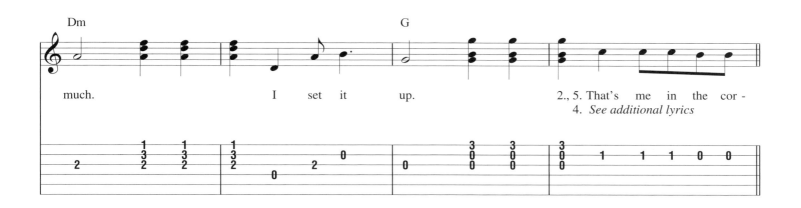

much.   I set it up.   2., 5. That's me in the cor -
4. *See additional lyrics*

%‌ Verse

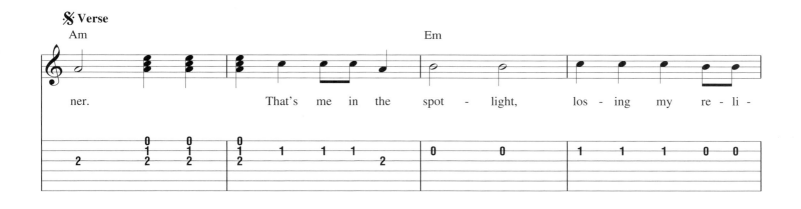

ner.   That's me in the spot - light, los - ing my re - li -

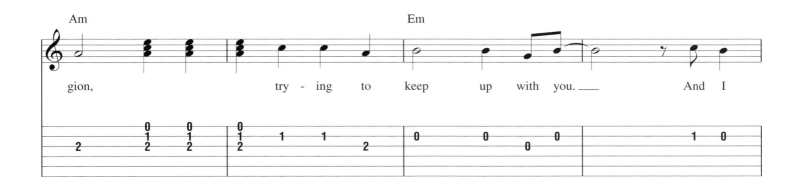

gion,   try - ing to keep up with you. ___ And I

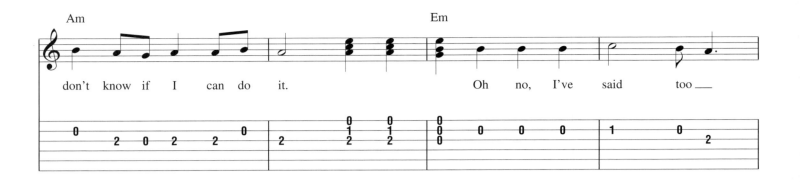

don't know if I can do it.   Oh no, I've said too ___

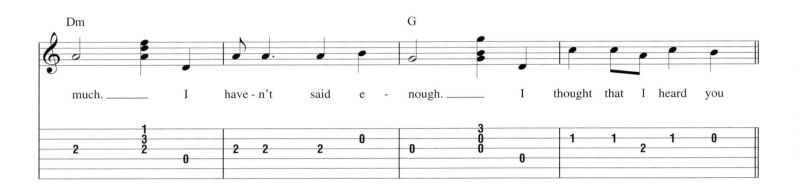

much. ___ I have - n't said e - nough. ___ I thought that I heard you

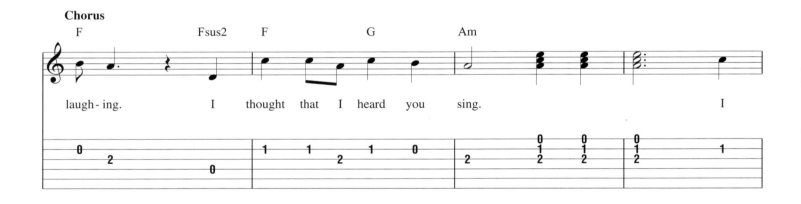

Chorus

laugh - ing.   I thought that I heard you sing.   I

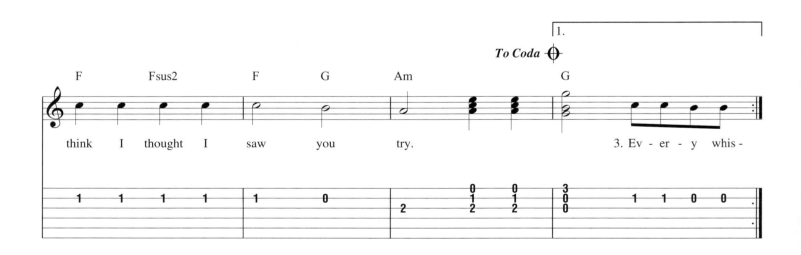

think I thought I saw you try.   3. Ev - er - y whis -

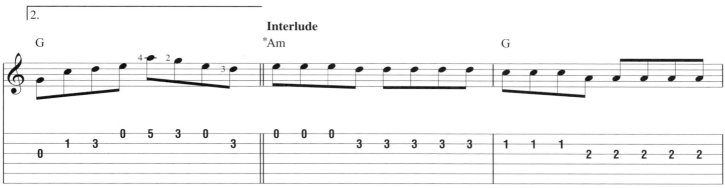

*Play chords once and let ring, next 8 meas.

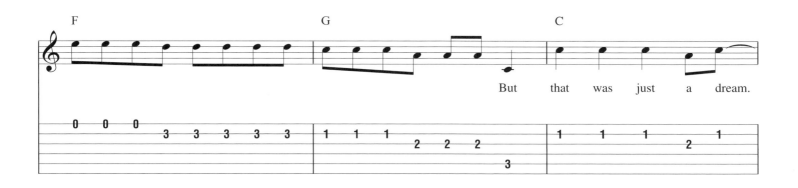

But that was just a dream.

D.S. al Coda

That was just a dream. __ 5. That's me in the cor -

Coda

But that was just a dream. __ Try. Cry. __

Why try? — That was just a dream, _ just a dream, _ just a dream,

Outro

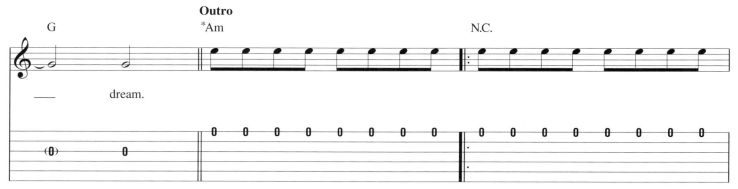

— dream.

*Play chord once and let ring.

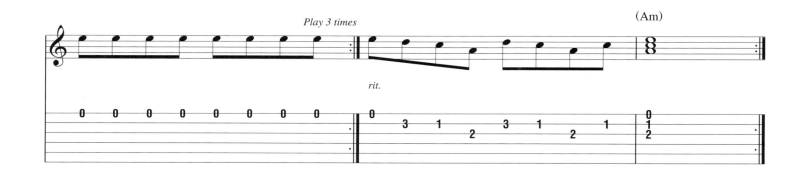

Play 3 times

rit.

(Am)

Additional Lyrics

2. Every whisper of ev'ry waking hour
   I'm choosing my confessions, trying to keep an eye on you,
   Like a hurt, lost and blind fool, fool.
   Oh no, I've said too much. I set it up.
   Consider this. Consider this, the hint of the century.
   Consider this, the slip that brought me to my knees, failed.
   What if all these fantasies come flailing around?
   Now I've said too much.

The One I Love

Words and Music by William Berry, Peter Buck, Michael Mills and Michael Stipe

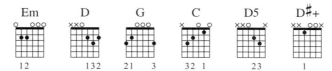

Strum Pattern: 1, 2
Pick Pattern: 2, 4

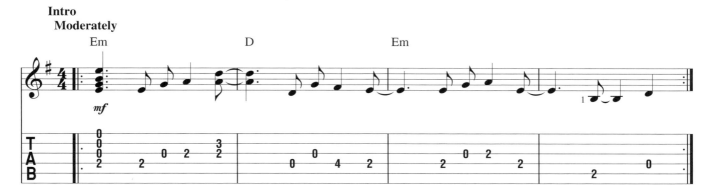

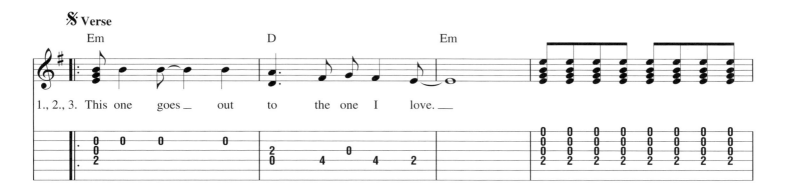

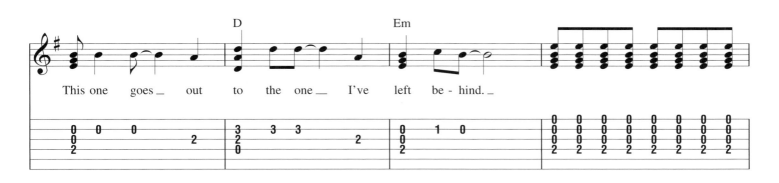

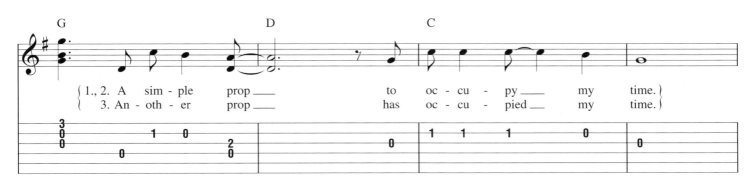

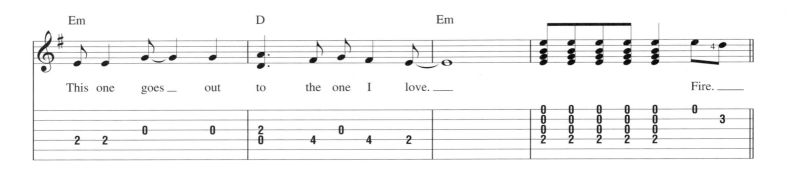

This one goes out to the one I love. ___ Fire. ___

Chorus

Fire. ___

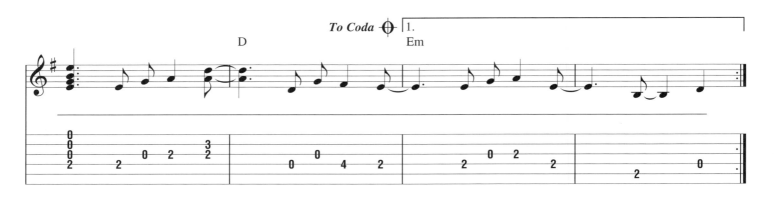

To Coda ⊕ 1.

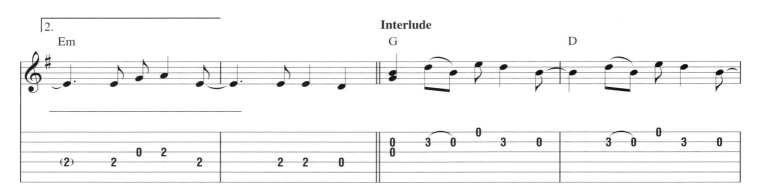

2.

Interlude

🜉 Coda

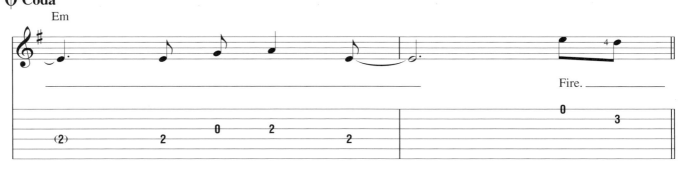

Fire.

Outro-Chorus

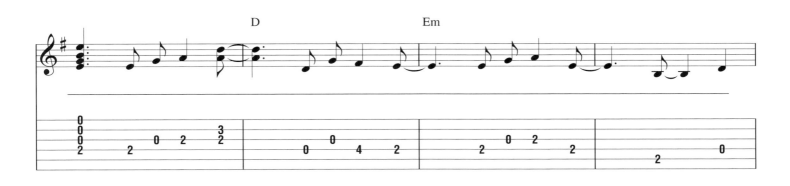

Fire.

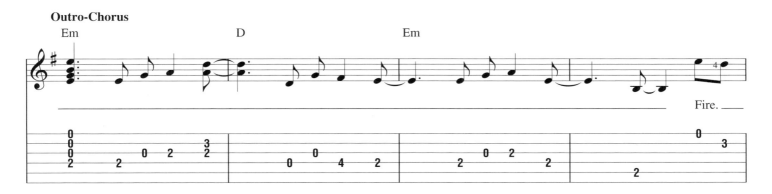

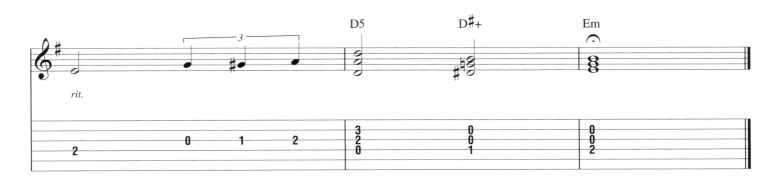

Man on the Moon

Words and Music by William Berry, Peter Buck, Michael Mills and Michael Stipe

Strum Pattern: 6
Pick Pattern: 4

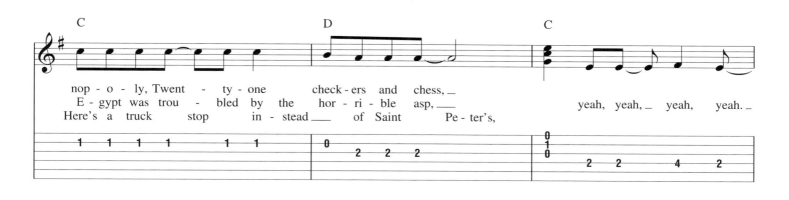

nop - o - ly, Twent - ty - one check - ers and chess, ___
E - gypt was trou - bled by the hor - ri - ble asp, ___
Here's a truck stop in - stead ___ of Saint Pe - ter's,

yeah, yeah, ___ yeah, yeah. ___

Mis - ter Fred Blas - sie in a break - fast mess, ___
Mis - ter Char - les Dar - win had the gall to ask, ___
Mis - ter An - dy Kauf - man's gone wres - tl - ing, ___

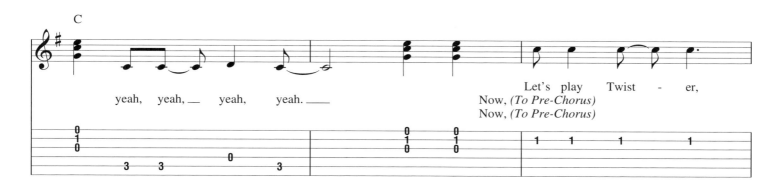

yeah, yeah, ___ yeah, yeah. ___

Let's play Twist - er,
Now, *(To Pre-Chorus)*
Now, *(To Pre-Chorus)*

let's play Risk, ___

yeah, yeah, ___ yeah, yeah. ___

I'll

see you in heav - en if you make the list, ___

yeah, yeah, ___ yeah, yeah. ___

Pre-Chorus

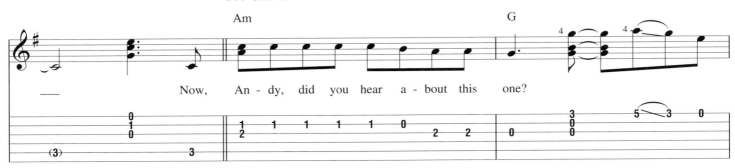

Now, An-dy, did you hear a-bout this one?

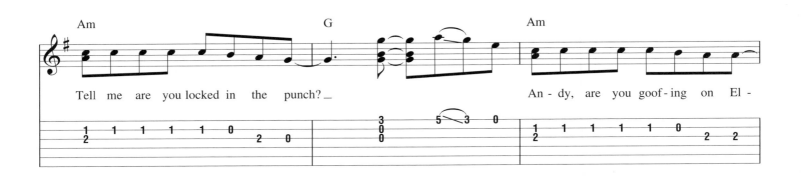

Tell me are you locked in the punch? _ An-dy, are you goof-ing on El -

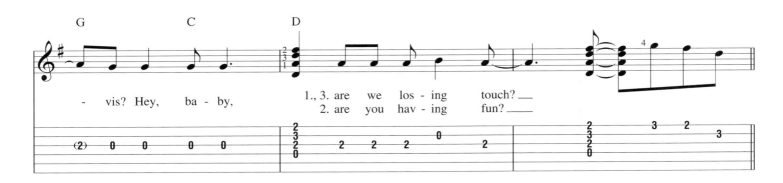

- vis? Hey, ba-by,   1., 3. are we los-ing touch? _
                        2. are you hav-ing fun? _

Chorus

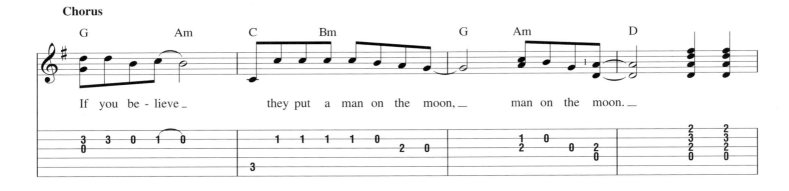

If you be-lieve _ they put a man on the moon, _ man on the moon. _

If you be-lieve _ there's noth-ing up their sleeve, _ then noth-ing is cool. _

Interlude

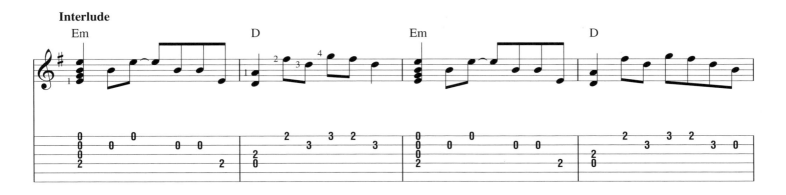

To Coda ⊕   D.S. al Coda
(no repeat)   ⊕ Coda

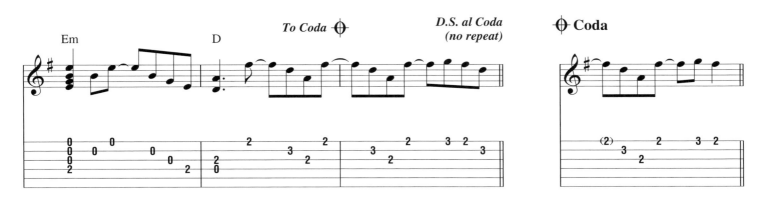

Outro-Chorus

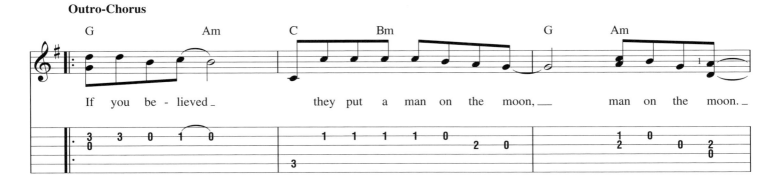

If you be-lieved __ they put a man on the moon, __ man on the moon. __

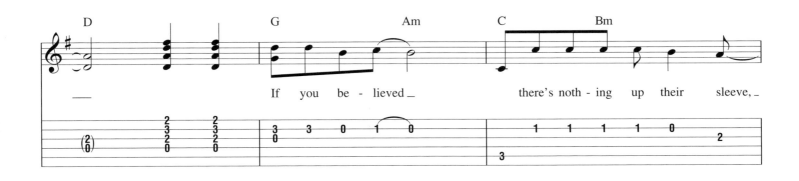

__ If you be-lieved __ there's noth-ing up their sleeve, __

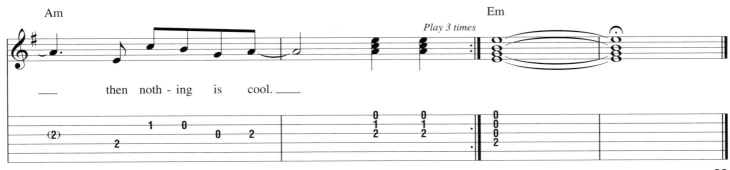

__ then noth-ing is cool. ____

Nightswimming

Words and Music by William Berry, Peter Buck, Michael Mills and Michael Stipe

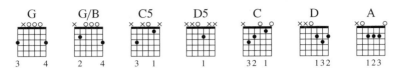

Strum Pattern: 6
Pick Pattern: 4

Intro
Moderately

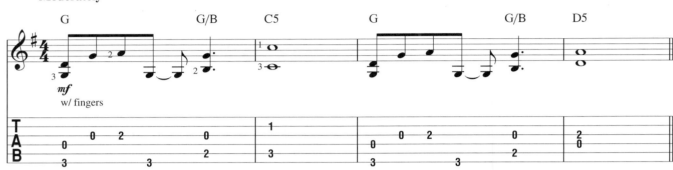

Verse

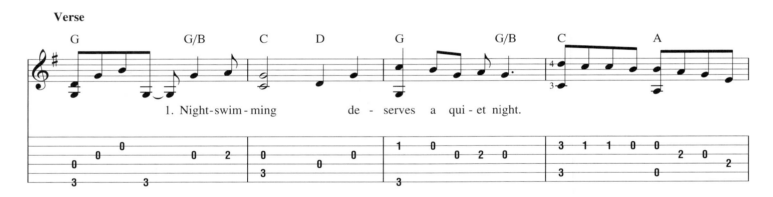

1. Night-swim-ming de - serves a qui - et night.

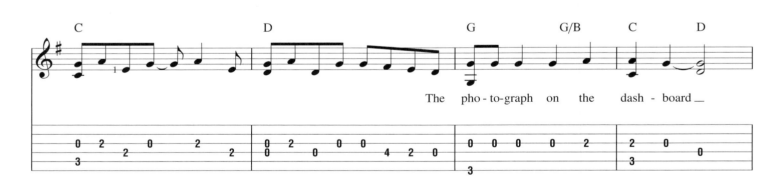

The pho-to-graph on the dash-board _

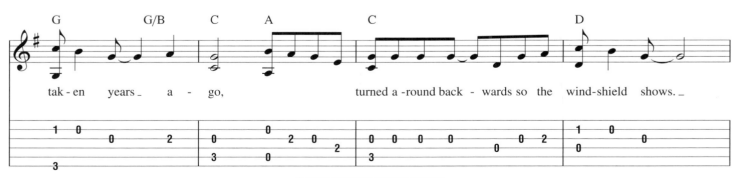

tak-en years _ a - go, turned a-round back - wards so the wind-shield shows. _

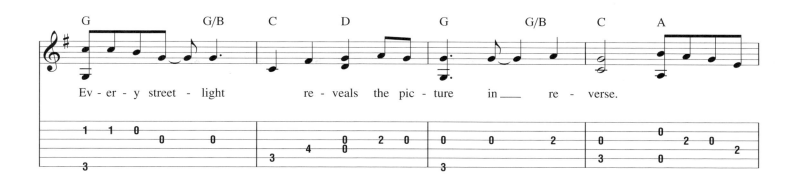

Ev - er - y street - light   re - veals the pic - ture   in ___ re - verse.

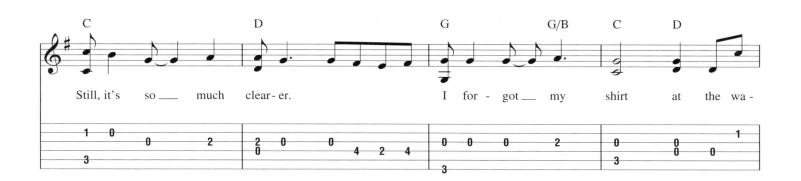

Still, it's   so ___ much   clear - er.   I for - got ___ my   shirt   at the wa -

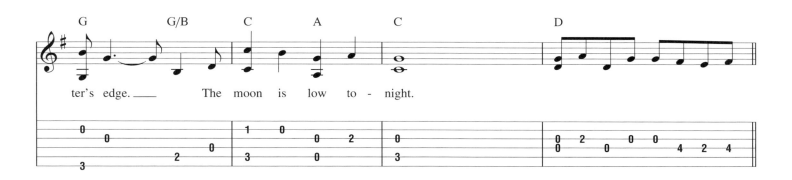

ter's edge. ___   The moon is   low to - night.

Interlude

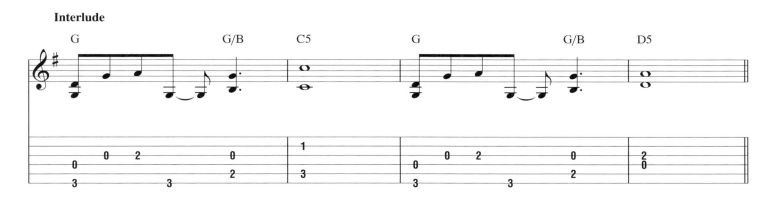

Verse

2. Night - swim - ming   de - serves a qui - et night.   I'm

not sure all these peo - ple un - der - stand._____ It's not like years a -

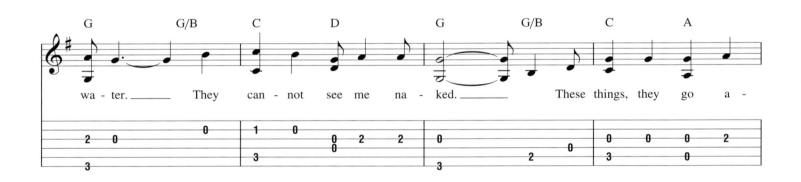

go,_____ the fear of get - ting caught,_____ of reck - less - ness___ and

wa - ter._____ They can - not see me na - ked._____ These things, they go a -

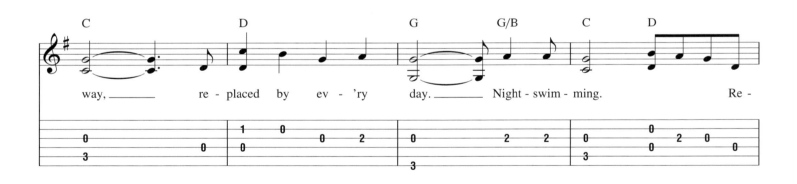

way,_____ re - placed by ev - 'ry day._____ Night - swim - ming. Re -

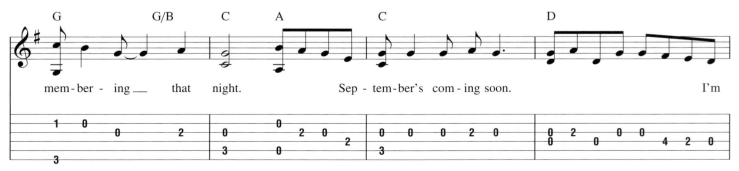

mem - ber - ing___ that night. Sep - tem - ber's com - ing soon. I'm

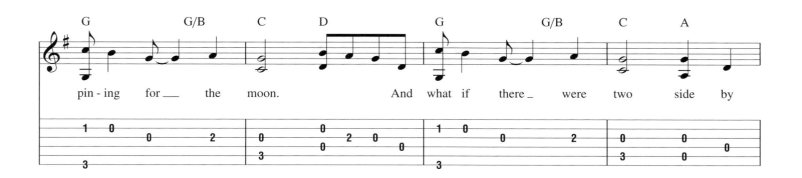

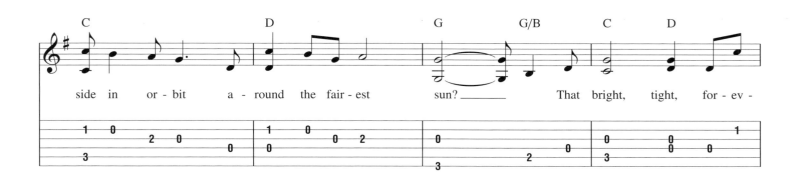

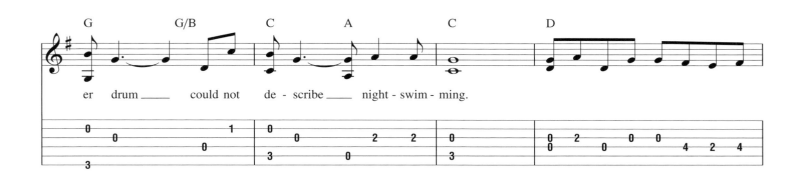

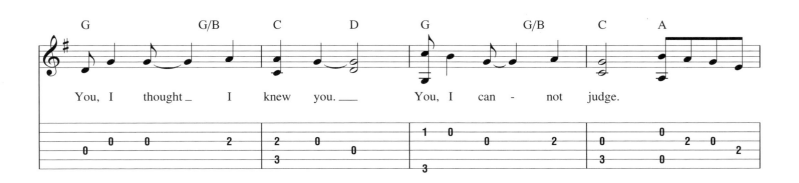

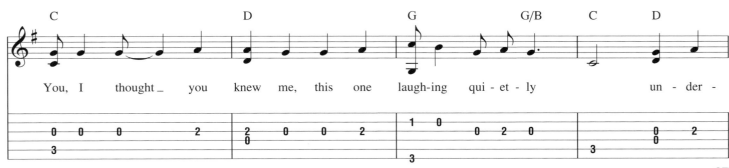

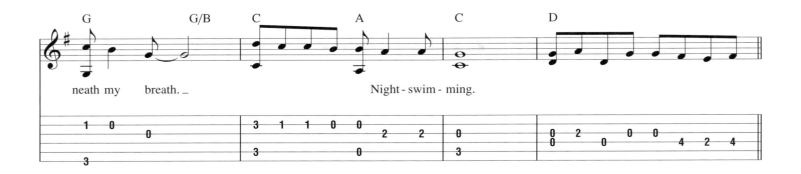

neath my   breath. _   Night - swim - ming.

Interlude

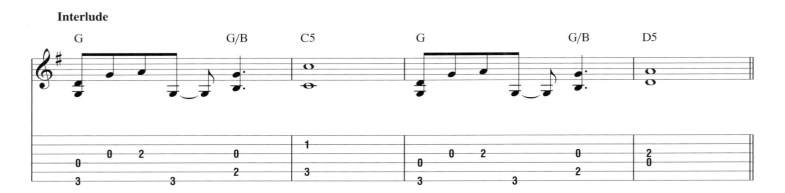

Oboe Solo

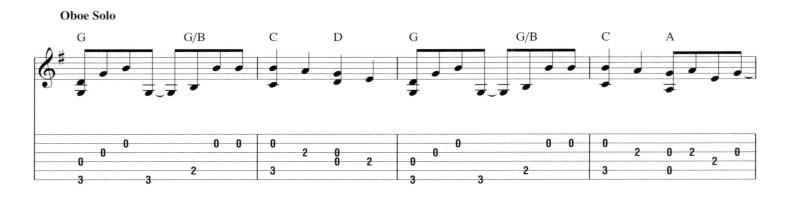

Verse

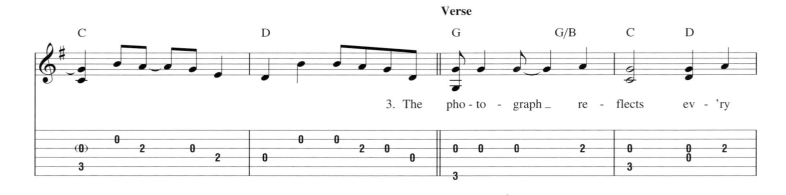

3. The   pho - to - graph _   re - flects   ev - 'ry

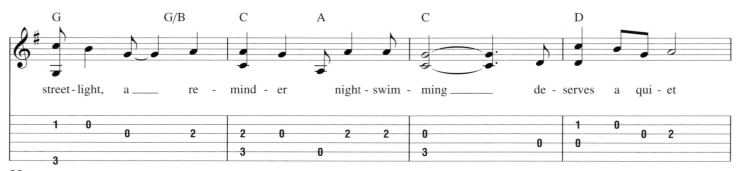

street - light,   a ____   re - mind - er   night - swim - ming _____   de - serves   a   qui - et

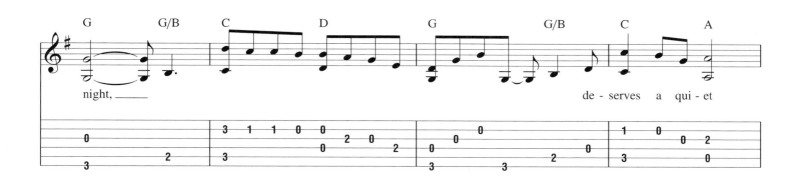

night, _____

de - serves a qui - et

Outro-Oboe Solo

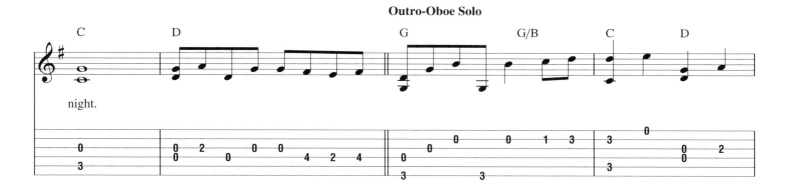

night.

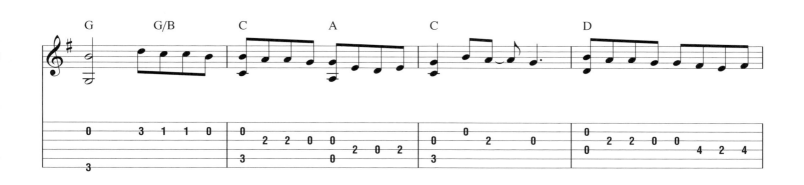

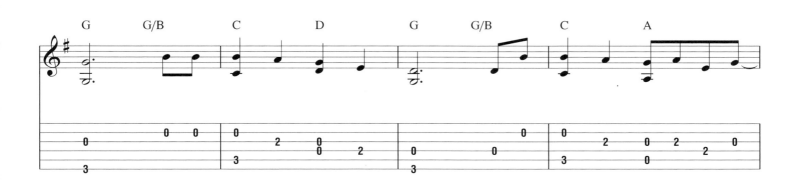

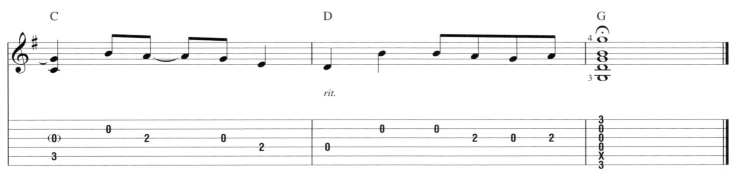

rit.

Orange Crush

Words and Music by William Berry, Peter Buck, Michael Mills and Michael Stipe

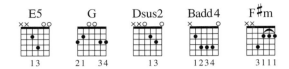

Strum Pattern: 6
Pick Pattern: 4

Intro
Moderately

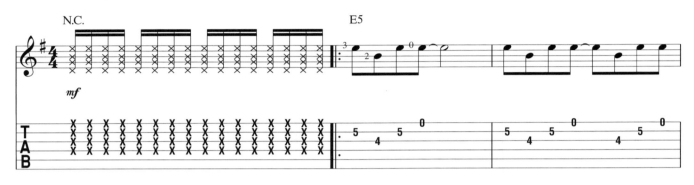

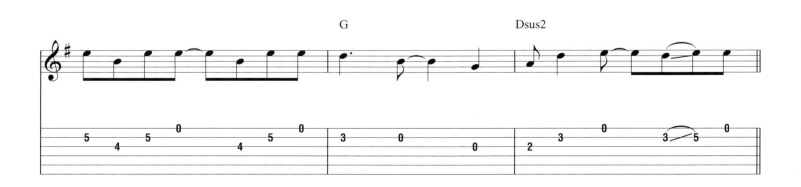

% Verse

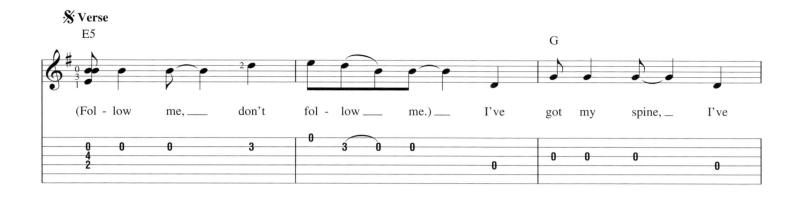

(Fol - low me, ___ don't fol - low ___ me.) ___ I've got my spine, ___ I've

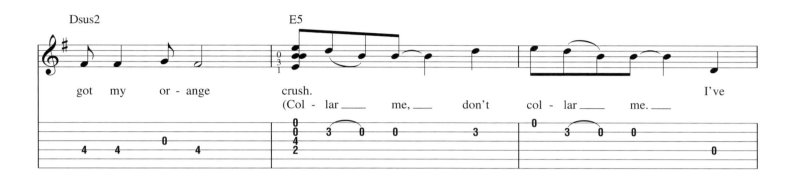

got my or - ange crush.
(Col - lar ___ me, ___ don't col - lar ___ me. ___ I've

got my spine, ___ I've got my or - ange crush.
We are a - gents

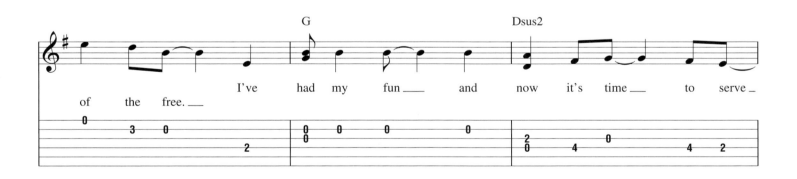

I've had my fun ___ and now it's time ___ to serve ___
of the free. ___

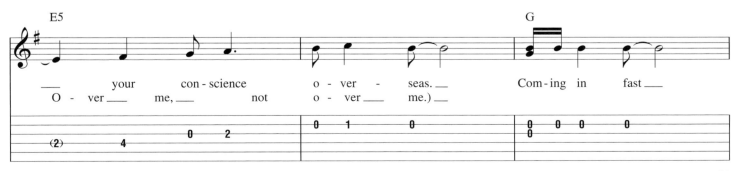

___ your con - science o - ver - seas. ___ Com - ing in fast ___
O - ver ___ me, ___ not o - ver ___ me.) ___

Bridge

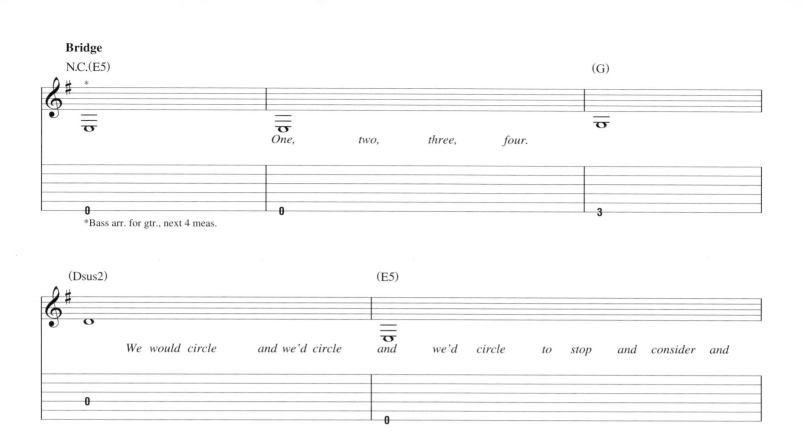

*Bass arr. for gtr., next 4 meas.

One, two, three, four.

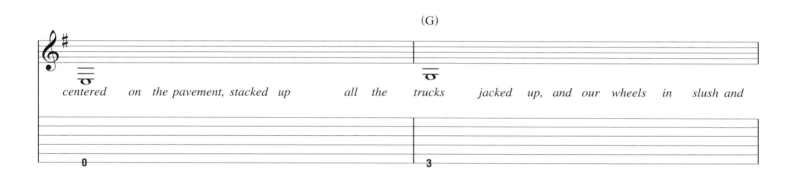

We would circle and we'd circle and we'd circle to stop and consider and

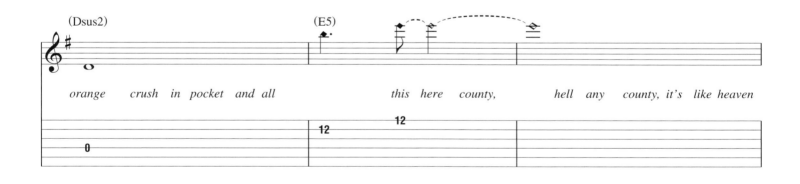

centered on the pavement, stacked up all the trucks jacked up, and our wheels in slush and

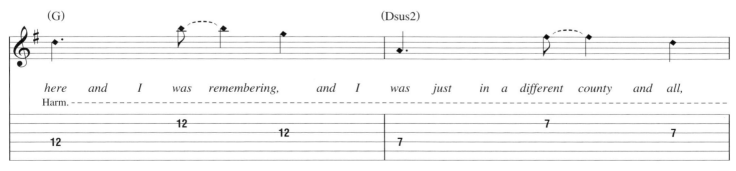

orange crush in pocket and all this here county, hell any county, it's like heaven

here and I was remembering, and I was just in a different county and all,

Harm.

then this whirlybird that I headed for, I had my goggles pulled off.

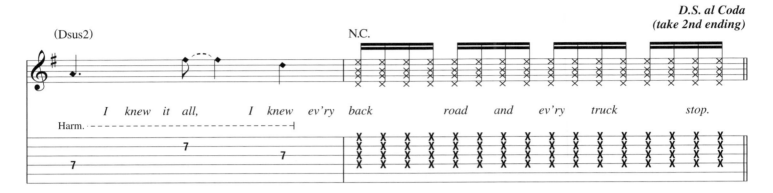

D.S. al Coda
(take 2nd ending)

I knew it all, I knew ev'ry back road and ev'ry truck stop.

⊕ Coda

Outro-Chorus

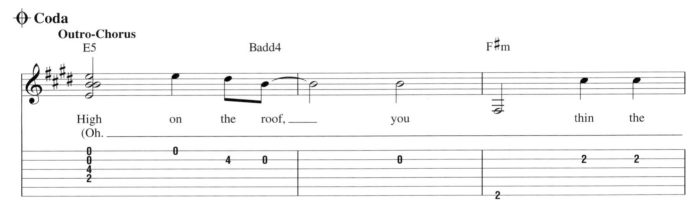

High on the roof, _____ you thin the
(Oh. ____

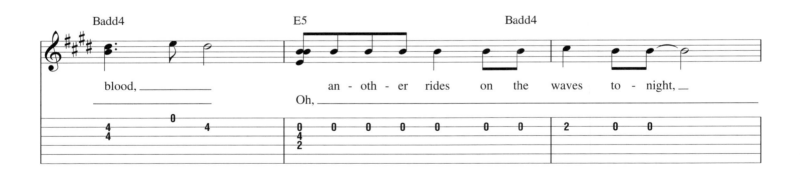

blood, _____ an - oth - er rides on the waves to - night, _____
Oh,

com - in' in - to your home. _____
oh.) ____

What's the Frequency, Kenneth?

Words and Music by William Berry, Peter Buck, Michael Mills and Michael Stipe

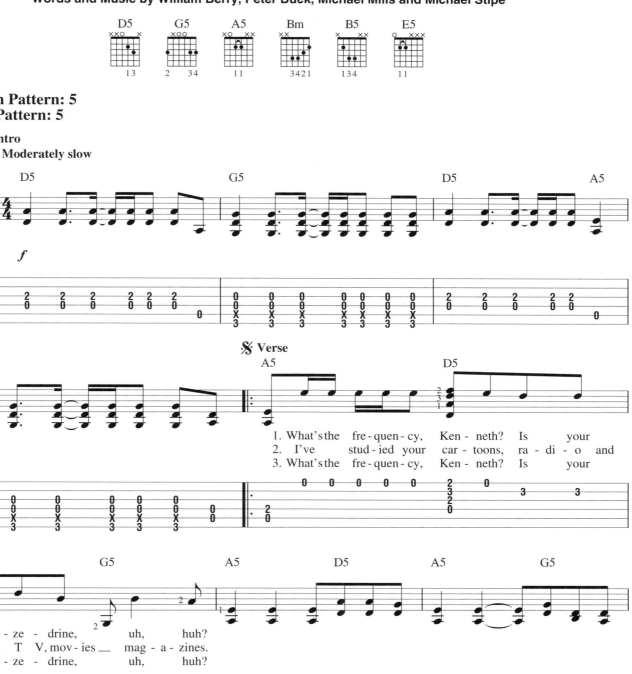

Strum Pattern: 5
Pick Pattern: 5

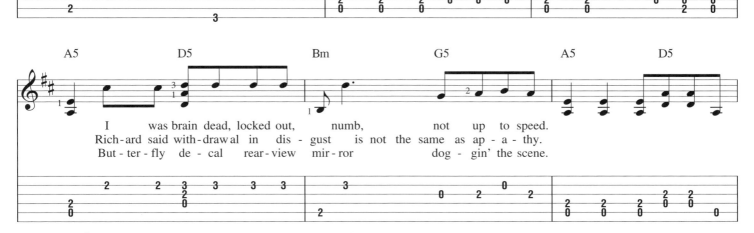

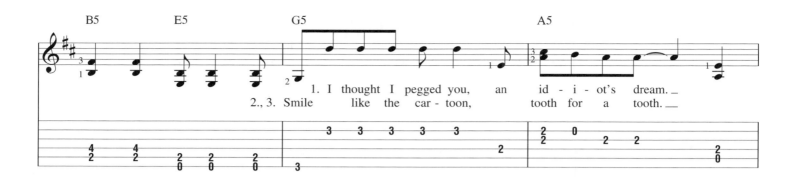

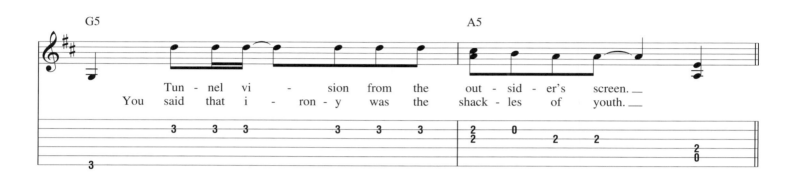

Chorus

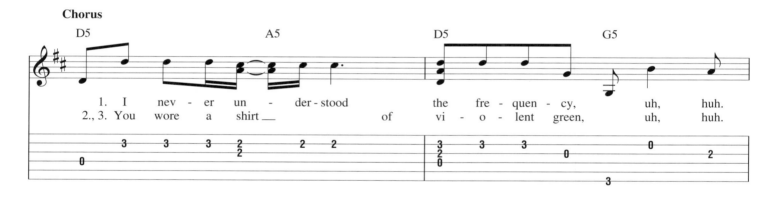

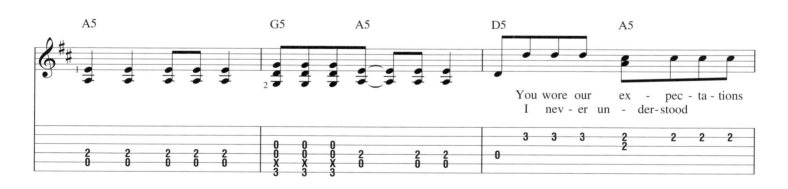

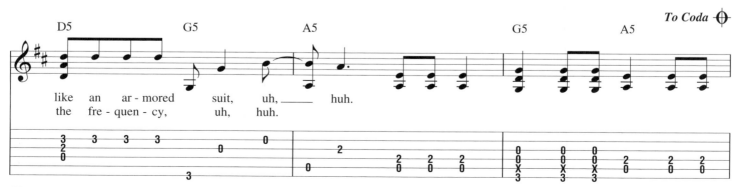

Shiny Happy People

Words and Music by William Berry, Peter Buck, Michael Mills and Michael Stipe

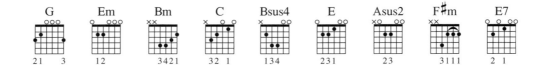

*Strum Pattern: 8
*Pick Pattern: 8

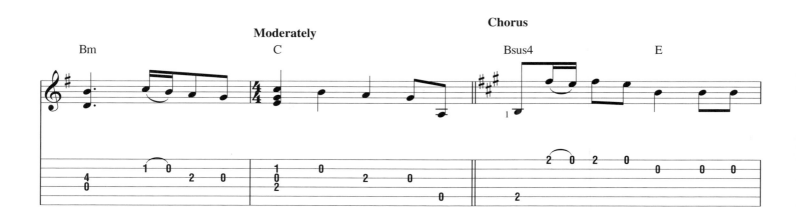

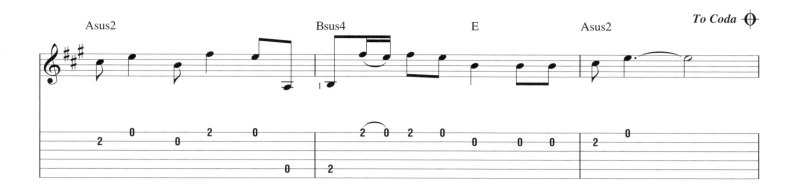

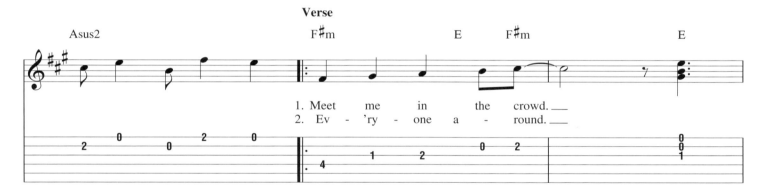

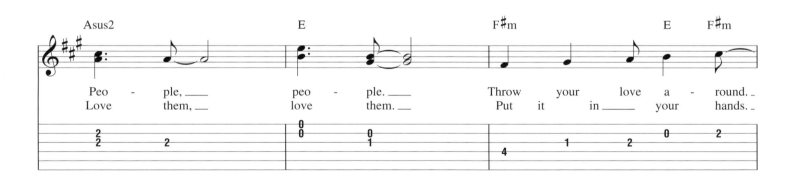

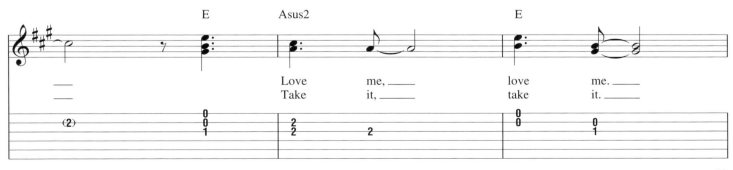

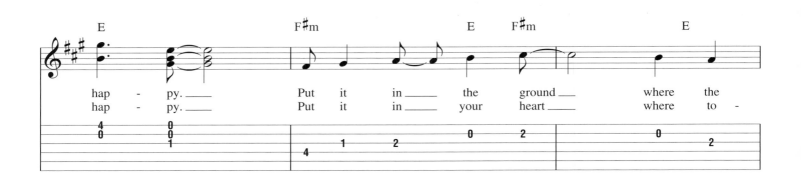

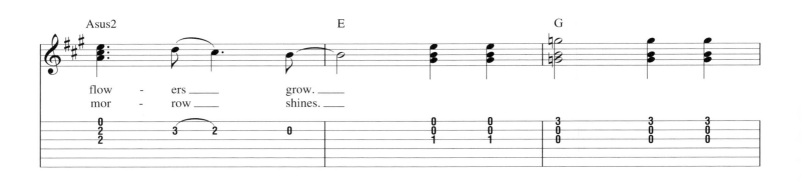

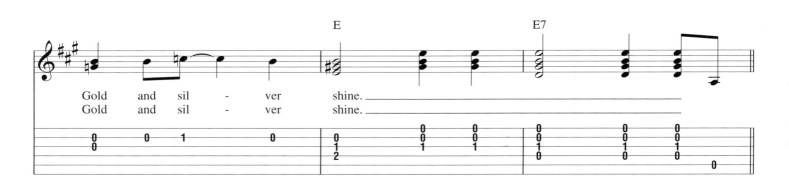

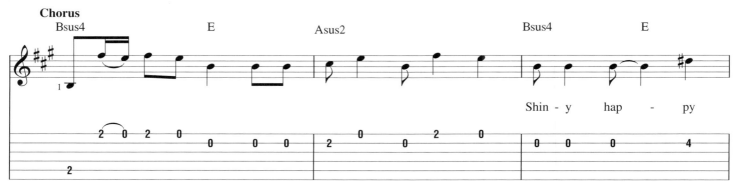

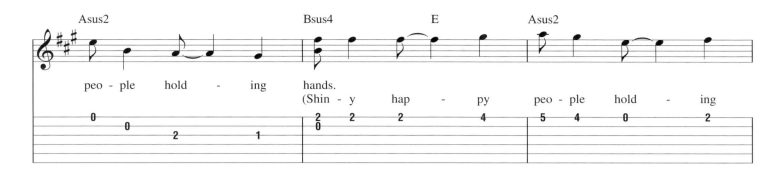

peo - ple hold - ing hands.
(Shin - y hap - py peo - ple hold - ing

D.C. al Coda

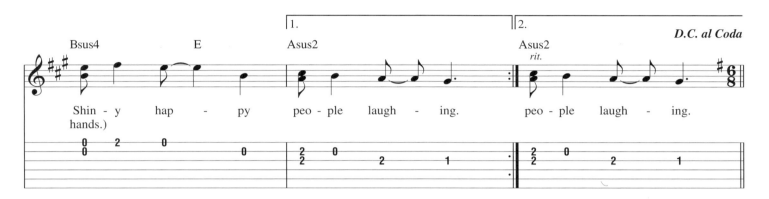

1. Shin - y hap - py peo - ple laugh - ing.
hands.)

2. peo - ple laugh - ing.

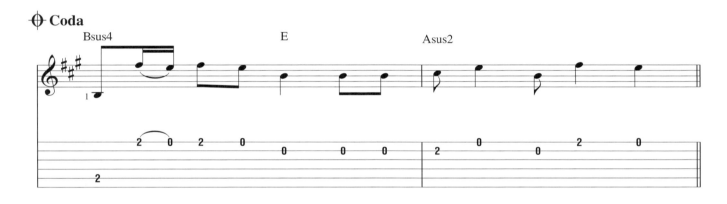

Coda

Outro-Chorus

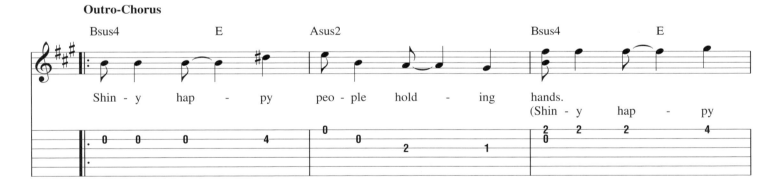

Shin - y hap - py peo - ple hold - ing hands.
(Shin - y hap - py

Repeat and fade

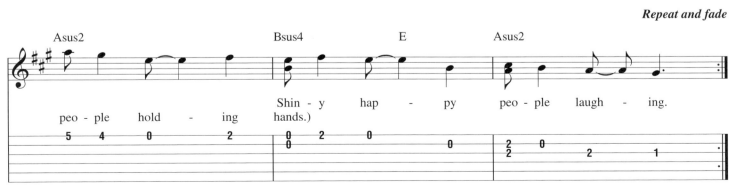

peo - ple hold - ing hands.
Shin - y hap - py peo - ple laugh - ing.

Stand

Words and Music by William Berry, Peter Buck, Michael Mills and Michael Stipe

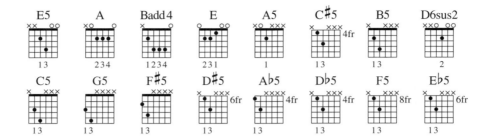

Strum Pattern: 3
Pick Pattern: 3

Intro
Moderately

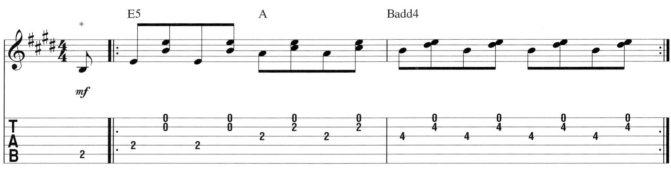

*Organ arr. for gtr., next 2 meas.

§ Chorus

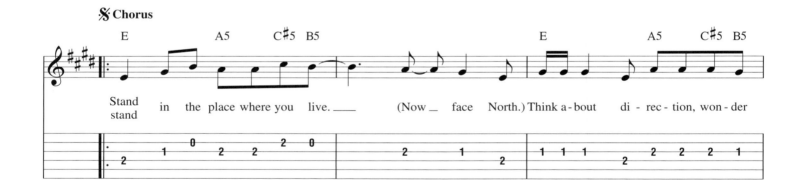

Stand
stand   in   the   place   where   you   live. ___   (Now ___ face North.) Think a-bout   di - rec - tion, won - der

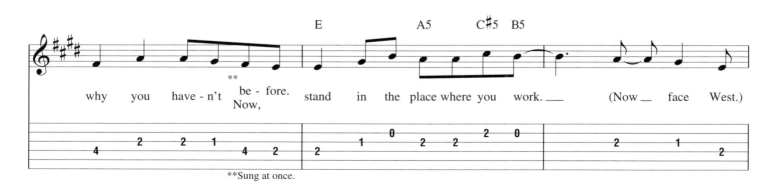

why   you   have - n't   be - fore.   stand   in   the   place   where   you   work. ___   (Now ___ face   West.)
Now,

**Sung at once.

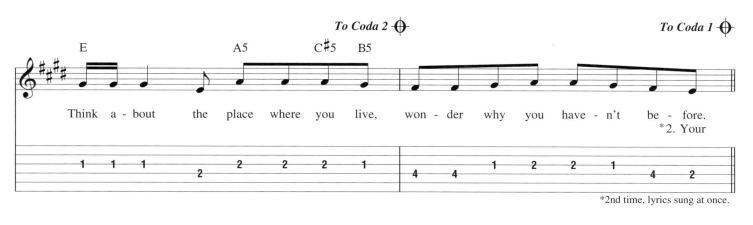
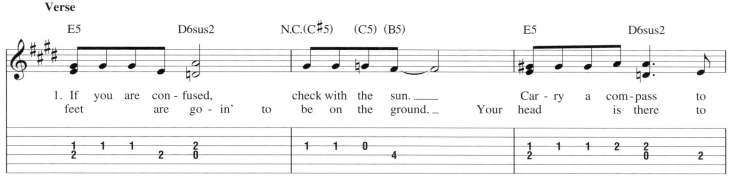
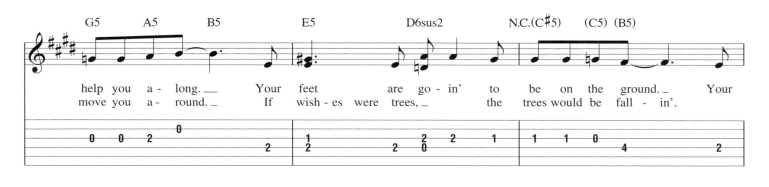
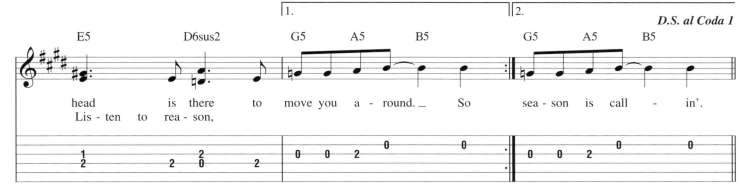
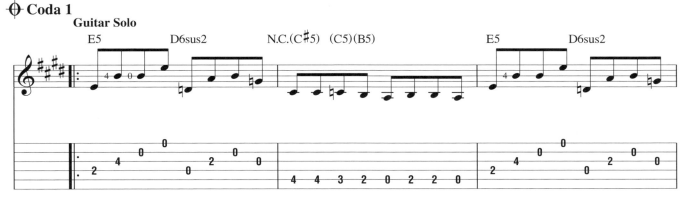

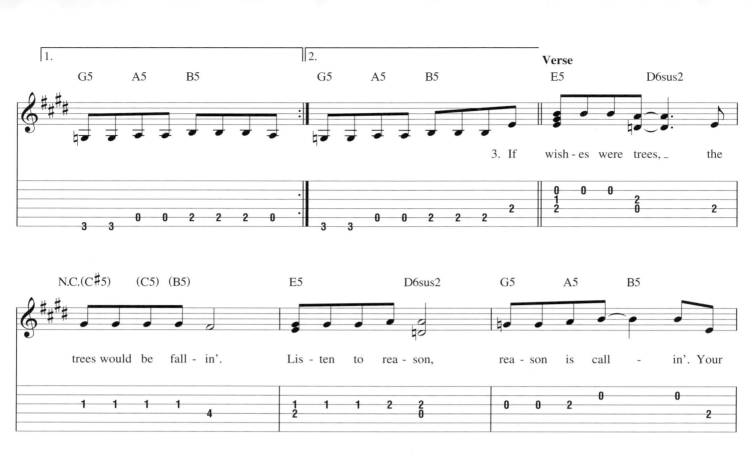

3. If wish-es were trees, _ the trees would be fall-in'. Lis-ten to rea-son, rea-son is call - in'. Your

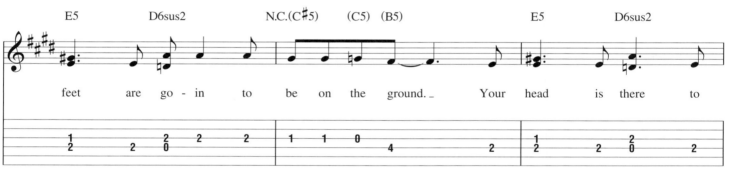

feet are go-in to be on the ground. _ Your head is there to

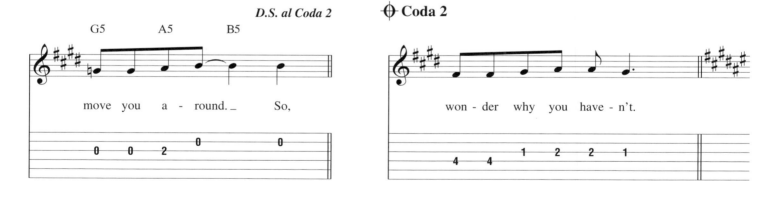

D.S. al Coda 2   **⊕ Coda 2**

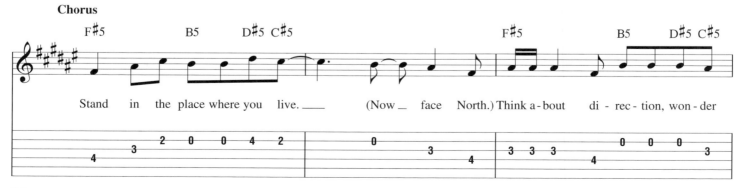

move you a - round. _ So,   won-der why you have-n't.

Chorus

Stand in the place where you live. _____ (Now _ face North.) Think a-bout di - rec - tion, won-der

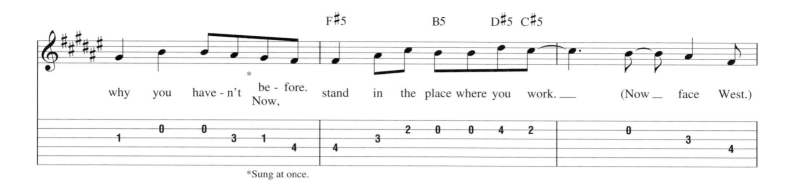

why you have-n't be - fore. Now, stand in the place where you work. ___ (Now ___ face West.)

*Sung at once.

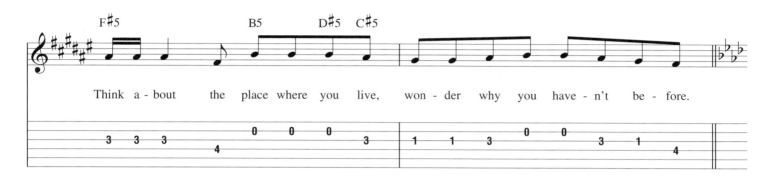

Think a - bout the place where you live, won - der why you have - n't be - fore.

Chorus

Stand in the place where you are. ___ (Now ___ face North.) Stand in the place where you are. _

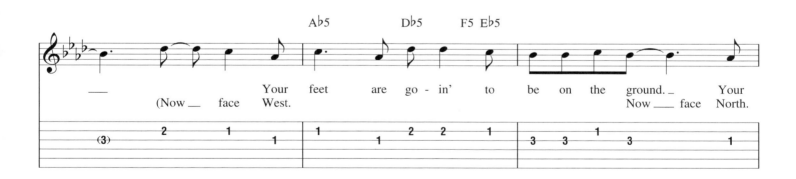

___ (Now ___ face West.) Your feet are go - in' to be on the ground. _ Your Now ___ face North.

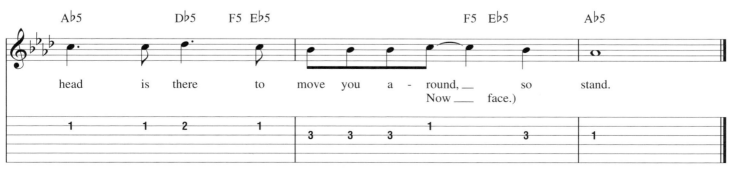

head is there to move you a - round, ___ so stand. Now ___ face.)

EASY GUITAR
WITH NOTES & TAB

This series features simplified arrangements with notes, tab, chord charts, and strum and pick patterns.

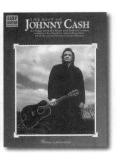

MIXED FOLIOS

00702287	Acoustic	$14.99
00702002	Acoustic Rock Hits for Easy Guitar	$12.95
00702166	All-Time Best Guitar Collection	$19.99
00699665	Beatles Best	$12.95
00702232	Best Acoustic Songs for Easy Guitar	$12.99
00702233	Best Hard Rock Songs	$14.99
00703055	The Big Book of Nursery Rhymes & Children's Songs	$14.99
00698978	Big Christmas Collection	$16.95
00702394	Bluegrass Songs for Easy Guitar	$12.99
00702149	Children's Christian Songbook	$7.95
00702237	Christian Acoustic Favorites	$12.95
00702028	Christmas Classics	$7.95
00702185	Christmas Hits	$9.95
00702016	Classic Blues for Easy Guitar	$12.95
00702141	Classic Rock	$8.95
00702203	CMT's 100 Greatest Country Songs	$27.95
00702283	The Contemporary Christian Collection	$16.99
00702006	Contemporary Christian Favorites	$9.95
00702239	Country Classics for Easy Guitar	$19.99
00702282	Country Hits of 2009-2010	$14.99
00702240	Country Hits of 2007-2008	$12.95
00702225	Country Hits of '06-'07	$12.95
00702085	Disney Movie Hits	$12.95

00702257	Easy Acoustic Guitar Songs	$14.99
00702280	Easy Guitar Tab White Pages	$29.99
00702212	Essential Christmas	$9.95
00702041	Favorite Hymns for Easy Guitar	$9.95
00702281	4 Chord Rock	$9.99
00702286	Glee	$16.99
00702174	God Bless America® & Other Songs for a Better Nation	$8.95
00699374	Gospel Favorites	$14.95
00702160	The Great American Country Songbook	$15.99
00702050	Great Classical Themes for Easy Guitar	$6.95
00702131	Great Country Hits of the '90s	$8.95
00702116	Greatest Hymns for Guitar	$8.95
00702130	The Groovy Years	$9.95
00702184	Guitar Instrumentals	$9.95
00702046	Hits of the '70s for Easy Guitar	$8.95
00702273	Irish Songs	$12.99
00702275	Jazz Favorites for Easy Guitar	$14.99
00702274	Jazz Standards for Easy Guitar	$14.99
00702162	Jumbo Easy Guitar Songbook	$19.95
00702258	Legends of Rock	$14.99
00702261	Modern Worship Hits	$14.99
00702189	MTV's 100 Greatest Pop Songs	$24.95
00702272	1950s Rock	$14.99

00702271	1960s Rock	$14.99
00702270	1970s Rock	$14.99
00702269	1980s Rock	$14.99
00702268	1990s Rock	$14.99
00702187	Selections from O Brother Where Art Thou?	$12.95
00702178	100 Songs for Kids	$12.95
00702515	Pirates of the Caribbean	$12.99
00702125	Praise and Worship for Guitar	$9.95
00702155	Rock Hits for Guitar	$9.95
00702110	The Sound of Music	$9.99
00702285	Southern Rock Hits	$12.99
00702866	Theme Music	$12.99
00702124	Today's Christian Rock – 2nd Edition	$9.95
00702220	Today's Country Hits	$9.95
00702198	Today's Hits for Guitar	$9.95
00702217	Top Christian Hits	$12.95
00702235	Top Christian Hits of '07-'08	$14.95
00702556	Top Hits of 2011	$14.99
00702294	Top Worship Hits	$14.99
00702206	Very Best of Rock	$9.95
00702255	VH1's 100 Greatest Hard Rock Songs	$27.99
00702175	VH1's 100 Greatest Songs of Rock and Roll	$24.95
00702253	Wicked	$12.99

ARTIST COLLECTIONS

00702267	AC/DC for Easy Guitar	$15.99
00702598	Adele for Easy Guitar	$14.99
00702001	Best of Aerosmith	$16.95
00702040	Best of the Allman Brothers	$14.99
00702865	J.S. Bach for Easy Guitar	$12.99
00702169	Best of The Beach Boys	$12.99
00702292	The Beatles – 1	$19.99
00702201	The Essential Black Sabbath	$12.95
00702140	Best of Brooks & Dunn	$10.95
02501615	Zac Brown Band – The Foundation	$16.99
02501621	Zac Brown Band – You Get What You Give	$16.99
00702095	Best of Mariah Carey	$12.95
00702043	Best of Johnny Cash	$16.99
00702033	Best of Steven Curtis Chapman	$14.95
00702291	Very Best of Coldplay	$12.99
00702263	Best of Casting Crowns	$12.99
00702090	Eric Clapton's Best	$10.95
00702086	Eric Clapton – from the Album Unplugged	$10.95
00702202	The Essential Eric Clapton	$12.95
00702250	blink-182 – Greatest Hits	$12.99
00702053	Best of Patsy Cline	$10.95
00702229	The Very Best of Creedence Clearwater Revival	$14.99
00702145	Best of Jim Croce	$12.99
00702278	Crosby, Stills & Nash	$12.99
00702219	David Crowder*Band Collection	$12.95
00702122	The Doors for Easy Guitar	$12.99
00702276	Fleetwood Mac – Easy Guitar Collection	$12.99

00702099	Best of Amy Grant	$9.95
00702190	Best of Pat Green	$19.95
00702136	Best of Merle Haggard	$12.99
00702243	Hannah Montana	$14.95
00702244	Hannah Montana 2/Meet Miley Cyrus	$16.95
00702227	Jimi Hendrix – Smash Hits	$14.99
00702288	Best of Hillsong United	$12.99
00702236	Best of Antonio Carlos Jobim	$12.95
00702245	Elton John – Greatest Hits 1970-2002	$14.99
00702204	Robert Johnson	$9.95
00702277	Best of Jonas Brothers	$14.99
00702234	Selections from Toby Keith – 35 Biggest Hits	$12.95
00702003	Kiss	$9.95
00702193	Best of Jennifer Knapp	$12.95
00702097	John Lennon – Imagine	$9.95
00702216	Lynyrd Skynyrd	$15.99
00702182	The Essential Bob Marley	$12.95
00702346	Bruno Mars – Doo-Wops & Hooligans	$12.99
00702248	Paul McCartney – All the Best	$14.99
00702129	Songs of Sarah McLachlan	$12.95
02501316	Metallica – Death Magnetic	$15.95
00702209	Steve Miller Band – Young Hearts (Greatest Hits)	$12.95
00702096	Best of Nirvana	$14.95
00702211	The Offspring – Greatest Hits	$12.95
00702030	Best of Roy Orbison	$12.95
00702144	Best of Ozzy Osbourne	$14.99
00702279	Tom Petty	$12.99

00702139	Elvis Country Favorites	$9.95
00702293	The Very Best of Prince	$12.99
00699415	Best of Queen for Guitar	$14.99
00702208	Red Hot Chili Peppers – Greatest Hits	$12.95
00702093	Rolling Stones Collection	$17.95
00702092	Best of the Rolling Stones	$14.99
00702196	Best of Bob Seger	$12.95
00702252	Frank Sinatra – Nothing But the Best	$12.99
00702010	Best of Rod Stewart	$14.95
00702049	Best of George Strait	$12.95
00702259	Taylor Swift for Easy Guitar	$14.99
00702290	Taylor Swift – Speak Now	$14.99
00702223	Chris Tomlin – Arriving	$12.95
00702262	Chris Tomlin Collection	$14.99
00702226	Chris Tomlin – See the Morning	$12.95
00702132	Shania Twain – Greatest Hits	$10.95
00702427	U2 – 18 Singles	$14.99
00702108	Best of Stevie Ray Vaughan	$10.95
00702123	Best of Hank Williams	$12.99
00702111	Stevie Wonder – Guitar Collection	$9.95
00702228	Neil Young – Greatest Hits	$15.99
00702188	Essential ZZ Top	$10.95

Prices, contents and availability subject to change without notice.

HAL•LEONARD® CORPORATION

7777 W. BLUEMOUND RD. P.O. BOX 13819 MILWAUKEE, WI 53213

Visit Hal Leonard online at
www.halleonard.com

0712